A PLACE TO STAND

WHEN LIFE THROWS YOU OFF BALANCE

MARK R. LITTLETON

MULTNOMAH · PRESS

Portland, Oregon 97266

Unless otherwise indicated, Scripture references in this volume are from the New American Standard Bible, © The Lockman Foundation, 1960, 1962, 1963, 1968, 1971, 1972, 1973, 1975, 1977. Used by permission.

Cover design and illustration by Al Mendenhall

A PLACE TO STAND
© 1986 by Multnomah Press
Portland, Oregon 97266

Printed in the United States of America

Library of Congress Cataloging-in-Publication Data
Littleton, Mark, 1950-
    A place to stand.

    1. Christian life—1960-   2. Bible—Bibliography.
I. Title.
BV4501.2.L564   1986   248.4   86-3041
ISBN 0-88070-141-2 (pbk.)

86 87 88 89 90 91 92 93 — 8 7 6 5 4 3 2 1

To Valerie, my wife,

God's great gift,

whose prayers, words, and life

have taught me and continue to teach me

much that is in this book.

Contents

God Wants Us to Stand!

When I was a Little Leaguer playing third base for Lyons' Sport Shop, I had to face a lot of twelve-year-old pitching maniacs. Some were wild. Some terrified me with glaring eyes and clenched teeth. Others pitched slowballs I was sure I could slam into the bleachers, and I would pray the coach would keep these in till I could bat.

But then there was Harvey B. He wasn't that fast, but he had mastered a number of breaking balls—curves, screwballs, knucklers, drops. I never knew what he was going to throw at me; I usually struck out when he pitched.

Frankly, I used to think of the Christian life that way. As a young Christian, I felt the Lord hurled some nasty curves into the circumstances of life. And often I struck out.

Do you ever feel that way? You're in good company. In this book you'll meet some of God's great creampuffs—people who, when the Lord began pitching, cried, "I can't handle this, Lord. Please stop."

As I've grown in the Christian life, I've discovered that while Harvey B. was planning to strike me out, God was planning something entirely different. He's more like a batting coach who wants us to learn to hit anything thrown at us.

Imagine you had such a coach. What's he going to do? First he'll warm you up with a few easy pitches you can wallop. Often the early Christian life is like that. Victory is easy. Everything moves quickly and securely toward the goal.

But the coach isn't interested in flinging only easy stuff. Later he begins throwing you harder pitches. At the same time he trains you to recognize such a pitch as it spins toward you from the mound. He shows you how to anticipate, set your bat, and swing through. In no time this coach will be throwing his hardest stuff at you—curves, sinkers, everything imaginable and worse. And his purpose is that you learn to hit them all!

Imagine that this coach is the greatest pitcher in history. No one in the league is better than he. If he teaches you everything he knows, you'll never face anyone who can strike you out. That kind of coach is going to produce some potent hitters, don't you think?

Now I have to admit I had rather limited talent as a baseball player. No matter how much coaching I got, I don't think I could've hit Harvey's curves or sinkers. I just didn't have what it takes. A lot of Christians will read this book and think that too. "Well, he writes a good line and it's interesting, but I don't think I really have it."

But let's suppose this incredible hitting coach is able not only to instruct, but also to crawl inside your body and stand in your skin at the plate. You'd still be in there, but he'd be in there too. He'd take hold of the bat through your hands, and not only show you how, but also do it in you.

And suppose this coach is not only the greatest pitcher who ever lived, but also the greatest batter—an unbeatable combination!

This is exactly what the Christian life is about. Our Lord not only wants to train us to hit anything that comes down the strike zone—from the world, the flesh, or the devil—but He'll also be inside of us, helping us gain the control we need to hit it.

This book, then, is about you and me as we stand at the plate and ready ourselves for the pitches life will hurl at us. It's about our cries in the dark, our moments of unbelief, the times of misunderstanding, failure, anger, laughter, and joy. It's about the curves, sinkers, and fastballs of life. It's about becoming like Jesus Christ, planting our feet, and standing firm so that when those pitches come, we're ready.

I've discovered that God isn't interested in producing just another winner, or slugger, or home-run king. There are plenty of them around. He's interested in making us so like Himself that we can stand up to anything.

That's where I'm headed. Will you join me?

Daddy, we've been learning about this man
in Sunday School. Moses.
Did you ever hear of him?
He was big and strong and he gave us
the Ten Commandments. Teacher says
he wrote lots of the Bible
and that he's almost as great as Jesus.
And he always did what God said.
Teacher says we should be like him
and obey God in everything we do.
Did you ever want to be like that, Daddy?
I'd like to be like Moses, Daddy.
I want to be strong like when he threw
down the stones with the Law on them
and everyone looked up and stopped dancing
because they knew he was mad
and they knew he meant business.
I want people to know when I mean business.
And teacher says when he was a little bitty
baby his mommy put him in the river
because they were going to kill him.
I don't remember why.
But I think that would be awful neat—
to be put in a river and be pulled out
by a princess, a real princess.
And teacher told us about how God
came to him in a burning bush, too.
Did you ever see God in a burning bush,
Daddy? That must really be something.
The only thing I don't understand
is that when God came in the burning bush,
Moses kept trying to get out of doing
what God wanted him to do.
Teacher said it was because he was scared,
but I don't believe it because

if God's as great as everyone says He is,
how could anyone be scared, especially
when God told him He was on his side?
If God told me that, I wouldn't be scared
of anyone. Nobody. Not even Billy Riggs
at recess or an arithmetic test or thunder
or anything. I wouldn't be scared of anyone.
Never. Not if God was on my side.
The only thing I'd be scared of
was not being on God's side.
Don't you think so, Daddy?
Don't you think so?

I

*M*oses:

"I'D RATHER NOT EVEN TRY"

Do you like "before and after" stories? How the lady goes from fat to fantastic in five easy lessons? Or how the skinny guy scurries off the beach after having sand kicked in his face, takes a Charles Atlas course, and comes back with biceps rippling?

These stories give us hope because all of us have weaknesses we wish would evaporate. Seeing someone who is down and out find the resources to stand up and win encourages us. "Maybe it could happen to me," we tell ourselves.

Such is the story of Moses. His problem was one all of us wrestle with: lack of confidence. He didn't think he could do anything right. He told himself he didn't have what it takes. Though he grew up a prince in Pharaoh's house, he made a mistake in his youth by killing a cruel Egyptian taskmaster. He wanted to free the enslaved millions of Israel. But he ended up a desert shepherd for forty years. Like any of us who have made a monumental error, he probably hacked away at his heart, calling himself a fool one minute and a criminal the next.

But God saw something deeper within this fragile man and appeared to him in a burning bush, summoning him to go to Egypt and free Israel from its slavery. Exodus 3 and 4 are the classic "Before" picture. God tells Moses to go, but he responds, "Who am I?" For a chapter and a half Moses and God argue. God tells him He'd be with him, and Moses says he can't do it. Moses finally ends the discussion by saying, "Please, Lord, send the message by whomever You like." In other words, "Pick anyone except me!"

This was one inferior-feeling fellow. But the story doesn't end there. God finally does get Moses moving, and only ten chapters later we read that he's standing on the edge of the Red Sea after having led more than two million slaves out of Egypt. Suddenly, dust rises in the distance. Hooves thunder in the air. People scream, "The chariots of Pharaoh! He's come to kill us all!" Panic surges through the crowd. Men move toward Moses. "You murderer! You brought us out here to kill us!" They're ready to heave him to Pharaoh as a peace offering.

What would Moses have done ten chapters ago? Probably shout to God, "I told you this would happen! I quit!" But not this Moses. He leaps onto a rock and shouts, "Do not fear! Stand up and watch God save you. He will fight Pharaoh while you keep silent."

Immediately, God speaks to Moses and tells him to stretch out his staff over the sea and move forward. Moses raises the staff and reaches out over the water. Instantly the air roars. The water rips back with an eerie suction. Suddenly a canyon the width of a hundred shoulders looms before them. The whole nation hurries through the chasm, and when Pharaoh tries to follow, Moses waves his stick again, and the sea claps together, drowning the Egyptians.

What a transformation! Where did this Moses come from? From being put through God's personalized program in confidence. The Lord built into his life that bold confidence that says, "God can do anything—so I'm with Him!"

Confidence. Do you have it?

It's what makes a football squad bound onto the field, energy surging. It's what keeps a housewife cool when the steaks burn and the husband is due in a minute. Without confidence a man is a marshmallow. With it, he's a rock.

WHAT CONFIDENCE IS

While many of us desire such confidence, it often eludes us. I can think of at least four kinds of confidence exhibited in our world today; only one smacks of spiritual power.

First, there's *self-confidence*. This is confidence generated from within. Muhammed Ali is it in technicolor. "I'm the greatest." No flinching. No trembling. Just rawbone certainty.

People lacking self-confidence often respond with *leader-confidence*. This is what we gain from hearing, seeing, or being with an able leader. Winston Churchill inspired such confidence. As he spoke his blood-bounding words over the radio waves of Britain, the Commonwealth pulsed with new vigor.

Still others find strength in *group-confidence*. This surfaces in the context of the crowd. Go to any pro baseball game and you'll see seat-sitters become rabble-rousers in the midst of the fanfare. We sense this in the camaraderie of a convention and the communion of a church. We draw strength from our peers and gain a sense of identity.

But all of these are inferior facsimiles of the real thing. They're generated from self or others like ourselves. If we or they crumble inside, we're done for. What all of us need is *God-confidence*. It comes from trusting God, knowing Him, walking with Him. Moses had God-confidence in Exodus 14 when he transformed defeat into victory. It's what he lacked in Exodus 3 and 4 when he tried to excuse himself from God's service at every command.

HOW GOD-CONFIDENCE IS DEVELOPED

But this brand of confidence doesn't come easily to the one seeking it. If you listen to the world, you'll hear several standard methods. "Develop a strong self-image." "Think positively." "Be tough." "Believe in yourself." "If you think you can, you can."

While this advice indicates that "self" can provide such confidence, most things that depend wholly upon human will or strength are destined for the slag heap. They're mere cosmetics unable to soothe spiritual pain. Outward action does not guarantee inward assurance. Cheerleading to the mind does not provide balm for the heart.

God-developed confidence enables a person to stand tall and granitic even when everyone else is buckling. Moses' story reveals five potent principles God uses to build confidence in people. As we apply them in the daily experiences of life, we'll begin to see that enduring confidence that keeps us plodding.

BY ASSURING US HE IS WITH US

God repeatedly assured Moses He was with him. Study the text. In 3:12, God said, "I will be with you." In 3:15 it's, "Thus you shall say to the sons of Israel, 'The LORD, the God of your fathers, the God of Abraham, the God of Isaac, and the God of Jacob, has sent me to you.'" In 3:18 He says Moses and the elders of Israel will tell Pharaoh, "The God of the Hebrews has met with us." In 3:20, God reiterates, "I will stretch out My hand." And in 4:12 He again asserts, "I, even I, will be with your mouth, and teach you what you are to say." All through the narrative, God prods Moses with such assurances. That's a primary principle: *Confidence comes when you know God is with you.*

This has always been God's way with His people. He speaks. We settle onto His words as upon concrete and wait till the truth hardens in our heart. Soon nothing can throw us.

It's amazing what happens to a person when he knows God is with him. When Martin Luther in 1521 stood before the Diet of Worms, a council that could burn him at the stake for his beliefs, he quietly told the priests, "Unless I am convinced by sacred Scripture or by evident reason, I cannot recant. For my conscience is held captive by the Word of God and to act against conscience is neither right nor safe. Here I stand; I can do no other, God help me. Amen." The religious world was flattened under the whirling wheels of this man's chariot for God.

Moses exhibited inextinguishable confidence because he knew God was with him. However, the idea that "God is with us" is often difficult for Christians to grasp. We wonder, "How can I be sure God is with me?" There are two keys to knowing God is with you. First, faith. Second, obedience.

Faith. "Without faith it is impossible to please God," (11:6) the author of the letter to the Hebrews said. But just as faith is the first step toward pleasing God, it's also the primary ingredient to experiencing God. Faith is the lens that focuses our eyes to see the truth.

In 2 Kings 6:8-19 the armies of Syria have surrounded Elisha and his servant Gehazi as they sleep in the city of Dothan. When Gehazi arises, he sees the smoke of their campfires, spies them from the wall, and begins crying, "What shall we do?" But Elisha is calm. He says, "Do not fear, for those who are with us are greater than those who are with them." Then he prays, "Lord, open his eyes that he may see." God answers. Instantly, the blinders fall off. Gehazi stares in wonder at the mountain flaming with the armies of God.

That's what faith does. Just as the eardrum picks up sound waves, and as pain sensors in our arms signal an infection or bruise, so faith is a sixth sense that enables us to see God—His presence, His love, His power, His greatness. As Moses exercised faith, he began to see more and more about God that built his confidence. As a result, when he stood on the edge of the Red Sea with Pharaoh galloping down on him, he did not give up. The chariots of Pharaoh meant nothing to him because he saw someone far greater: God. He knew God's power, and he was confident God would save them.

Obedience. However, faith minus obedience leads nowhere. But when you believe scripturally as Moses did, you begin to obey. At the same time, obedience leads us back to greater and deeper faith.

It happens like this. You read God's word and discover a new teaching you've never known. So you say, "It looks good on paper, but does it work?" You decide to exercise faith. Then an opportunity comes along and you apply the truth you learned earlier. Later when you reflect on what happened, you see how the scriptural principle did work and your faith is strengthened. You decide to find more principles and apply more truth as you go along. Your faith grows each time you obey what you believe.

That's what happened to Moses. God would give a command. Moses would obey. When he saw the principle worked out in reality, his faith was built.

This should be happening to us all the time. I was at work one afternoon struggling with a computer problem which made it impossible for me to run several important reports. All afternoon I tried different methods, called the computer help center, and read the reference books. But the computer was stuck. The next morning I had a meeting with my businessmen's Bible study. Suddenly it occurred to me that I hadn't even prayed about the situation. Matthew 7:7 came to mind. "Ask and you shall receive". I asked the men to pray. Shortly after I arrived in the office, I went to the computer and prayed again. The moment I finished, an idea struck me. When I tried it, the whole problem was clarified and I had the report running in a few minutes. I found myself saying, "I knew God understood IBM, but I didn't think He could work this fast!" My faith was built as I obeyed God's command. I saw once again God was with me and my confidence was enlarged.

BY TEACHING US TO OBEY DESPITE OUR FEELINGS

As Moses exercised faith in God and recognized that He was with him, a second principle began to work in his life: *When we learn to obey God despite our feelings, our confidence in Him grows.*

The walk of faith is strewn with many negative feelings. Moses repeatedly visited Pharaoh to ask him to let the people go, but Pharaoh only mocked him. Moses would stagger back to God and plead for another job. Nonetheless, God would tell Moses to go back—and Moses would go. He learned to obey despite his feelings. Learning to obey even when we are apprehensive about it builds confidence like nothing else. We discover that real confidence is based on God and His word.

We often think of confidence as this gutsy bravado, this inner feeling of strength that leads us to believe "I can take on the world." But such maniacal inner assurance can often lead to disaster. Confidence isn't a feeling; it's a conviction founded on truth.

Two opposite examples from my life come to mind. One is from my wrestling days when I had to go up against a skinny fellow who looked like he'd drop at a sneeze. I "felt" confident as I walked out onto the mat. In fact, I felt like Superman. Then we started wrestling. Suddenly, this skinny twerp turned into Tarzan of the Matmen. I was trounced.

On the other hand, I once had to preach a sermon in seminary before two well-known evangelists and the chairman of the preaching department. I was ready to trade in my sheepskin for a loincloth. But as I waited, I prayed and told the Lord, "Okay, You're on. If You don't come through, I'm cooked." I launched into my message and it went extremely well. Afterward several of the young men present commented at how poised I looked. They even wanted to know where I got such confidence!

The Lord longs that we learn to obey even though our feelings are bleak. The more we learn to obey because He commanded it rather than because we "feel like it," the more confidence we'll have that He'll work through us.

Such obedience isn't an option.

Still, many Christians look at obedience to God as though it is an option based on personality or past problems. One says, "My Mom was mean to me, Lord, so please excuse me if I just can't do it Your way now and then." Another person tells Him, "I've had a rough day, Lord, so just let me steam and sulk for a while." But God never compromises. He says, "Do as I say. Nothing else is acceptable."

When Moses struggled with his feelings, God didn't say, "I know you've been through the mill, Moses. So don't worry about it. Just do what you can!" When Moses shouted to Him, "I quit!" the Lord didn't hang His head and say, "Oh, I'm sorry I messed things up for you. Let me try it again!" No, God spoke and Moses obeyed. When he did fail, God replied, "Okay, I forgive you. Now try again and obey Me to the letter!" Gradually, Moses learned to obey no matter how badly he felt or things looked.

When we're young and immature, our feelings often overwhelm us. We make poor decisions because our feelings are so influential. We need to remember that God-confidence is learned. It comes with maturity in our walk with Jesus. It's not that some have it and others don't. Rather, it's an inner attitude that comes with disciplined fellowship with the Lord. If you find today that you have little to no confidence, don't berate yourself. Simply say, "Lord, help me grow in this area. Lead me into Your truth. Train me in confidence." He will. As we learn to obey despite feelings, gradually new and better feelings come that bear the fragrance of righteousness.

BY SHOWING US WHAT'S AHEAD

But again, this was not the end of God's work in Moses. He desired to develop in him the kind of confidence that exhibited courage, boldness, endurance, and hope. A third principle is illustrated in the life of Moses: *Knowing what's ahead and that God will provide insight along the way develops confidence.*

Over and over in the text we find God telling Moses what was coming. "Pharaoh won't listen." "The people won't believe." "I will perform signs." More than that, God informed Moses of what to do when things went wrong. Moses had a personalized answering service that delivered eternal wisdom on every subject.

Today because of the Scriptures we have information about everything—life, death, salvation, victory, power, love, patience, perseverance. We have the divine line on every issue imaginable. As Paul said, "All Scripture is inspired by God and profitable for teaching, for reproof, for correction, for training in righteousness; that the man of God may be adequate, equipped for every good work" (2 Timothy 3:16-17).

We gain that adequacy, that confidence, in facing every situation by knowing God's word—letter perfect. It's got to get embedded in our hearts. We need a growing inventory of verses and truth. That's why memorizing Scripture is so critical to growth. The Bible is like a dark house. At first it's a mystery. You wonder who or what will leap out at you if you open the wrong door. You jolt upright in bed when you hear a sudden bump in the night. But as you become familiar with the house, you no longer have to feel your way around, wondering what strange furry thing you'll touch next. You can settle down into the easy chair, pull a lemonade out of the fridge, or flick on the stereo without a care. As you study God's principles and prophecies, as you memorize them and chisel them into your soul, your confidence soars because you're certain God will guide you through life's tremors and quakes.

BY TEACHING US TO TRUST HIM

As we read how God informed Moses of what was ahead, we must remember God is sovereign. He exercises absolute control over every event in history. As a result, God began using the circumstances of life to train His prophet. Everything that happened to Moses was used by

God for his training and development. That brings out a fourth principle on the issue of confidence: *God uses the problems of life to teach us to seek Him and rely on Him for all situations.*

Repeatedly Moses found himself in circumstances he couldn't overcome by mere brain or brawn. For instance, in Exodus 5:20-21 the foremen of Israel come back from Pharaoh, having just learned their brick quotas would remain the same, though they were not receiving supplies of straw. When they see Moses, they begin yelling: "May God judge you for turning Pharaoh against us!" Moses' reaction was to run to God and tumble before Him, crying, "I can't take any more of this, Lord. Please let me do something else."

Now why did God allow this? To teach Moses to rely on Him alone. God gave Moses God-sized problems so Moses would be forced to rely on God. If God had given him man-sized problems, Moses would have been tempted to deal with them on his own.

As we learn not to rely on common sense, experience, or instinct, but to go to the Lord, open His word, and search for His answer, we find He proves trustworthy every time and our faith and confidence grow. Therefore, expect that God will shove you into circumstances that defy simple solution. Expect crises, problems, persecutions and frustrations to bounce into your life like rabid kangaroos. You not only *may* have a rougher time than most non-Christians, you *will*. How else will you become like Christ?

Let me tell you about my first year of marriage. Before I became a Christian at twenty-one, I desired to find a beautiful wife. When I met the Lord, I was sure He'd provide one. Pronto! But I had to wait eleven years. It was a good wait. Valerie and I were to be married on February 12, 1983. Unfortunately, on February 10 the monster snowstorm of the century hit Maryland. Our wedding was postponed to February 14, Valentine's Day. A nice twist, I thought, and thanked the Lord anyway. However, only half the people invited were able to come.

A month after settling into our apartment, Valerie became so sick one evening that we sped for the emergency room. We discovered she was pregnant—and suddenly I realized we didn't have health insurance. When we were finally accepted into a group plan, it was four months too late. We were told we'd have to foot the doctor bills. I tried to be optimistic. We could handle the usual $3,000 or so of a typical birth.

Two months before delivery, Valerie was stricken with toxemia. She ended up in the hospital again for two weeks. Unable to end her illness, the doctors wanted to go ahead with a Caesarean section. Otherwise both she and the baby could die. Nicole was born six weeks premature, weighing four pounds, and was put into the hospital's special care unit.

The day they were to go home, the accounts manager took me into his office. He informed me I owed the hospital $17,000. Though insurance would cover the baby's complications (about $5000), something had to be done. (It crossed my mind that I might become an indentured servant. But I had no hospital skills.)

It was a rough year. Our daughter was in danger of Sudden Infant Death Syndrome and for four months had to be on a machine monitoring her heart and breathing rate. We were awakened night after night with its loud beeping telling us she had stopped breathing. At the same time the church I was pastoring was undergoing some terrific problems and pressures. The situation finally led me to resign my position without another job in sight. We concluded the year with no job, still more than ten thousand dollars in bills, and a high-risk baby.

Yet one afternoon as we talked about our circumstances, I asked Valerie, "What do you think God is trying to do?"

She replied, "Oh, He's just teaching us to trust Him." I had to pinch myself at first. But I see it clearly now. Did the Lord prove trustworthy? Let me tell you after we consider one last principle.

BY SHOWING US HIS POWER

When things got this bad for Moses, God began using one last principle to bolster his confidence: *Through seeing God's power at work in our own problems, we become confident that we can face anything.* All through the narrative of the plagues, God sounds a refrain: "That they may know that I am the Lord." God displayed His power to show Moses, Israel, and Egypt just what He could do.

Meanwhile something else was happening within Moses. From Exodus to Deuteronomy he's undergoing a metamorphosis—from a piteous whimperer of excuses to a potent worshiper of God. In Exodus 3:5, Moses was so stuck in self-conscious muck that God had to order him to take off his shoes. But by the time we get to Exodus 33:18, Moses is sprinting after God. "Show me Thy glory," he cries. He wanted to know God through to the heart.

It was in Exodus 34 that Moses saw the "Finale of finales of the King of kings." God hid Moses in the cleft of the rock and marched before him in one incredible display of power. But what was it that God demonstrated? Not just physical fireworks! Moses had seen all that in the ten plagues and the many miracles in the wilderness. No, what God displayed was His perfect character. He said, "'The LORD, the LORD God, compassionate and gracious, slow to anger, and abounding in lovingkindness and truth; who keeps lovingkindness for thousands, who forgives iniquity, transgression and sin; yet He will by no means leave the guilty unpunished, visiting the iniquity of fathers on the children and on the grandchildren to the third and fourth generations'" (34:6-7).

Moses' reaction to those words was like a poverty-stricken goldminer discovering the Rocky Mountain Lode. He "made haste to bow low to the earth and worship" (34:8). For the first time he really saw who God is—not just a repository of power and amazing wonders; no longer merely a leader and general; but God, the living God, the Perfect One, awe-inspiring, powerful beyond description,

Potentate of the galaxies, Mastermind of the universe. Could anyone who sees God's power like that not worship Him and overflow with confidence?

MY SITUATION

That's exactly what I discovered in my circumstances. As we pondered our bills, we prayed. Suddenly over the next few weeks, checks from churches, friends, relatives, and others began pouring in. We received many for $100 to $300, several for $500, and one for $1,000, given anonymously. We were able to pay off all the due bills and arrange a payment plan with the hospital.

Our daughter lived through the risk period and now at two years old provides commentary on such things as this book by tearing it up, sitting on it, and so forth.

After I resigned from my position as pastor, I knew I needed a job fast. I went to my father, told him the situation, and asked him if he had anything in his company. "Let me think about it," he said, and within a week he came up with a perfect position for me as long as I needed it. In addition, his company provided me with after-hours access to a computer on which this book was written.

But even more than that, we saw the Lord Himself—His love, His loyalty, His unerring wisdom. I felt as though I was in the cleft of that rock seeing God pass by. I began to realize there was nothing in this world to fear except sin, and no one in all the universe to fear except Him.

That's confidence. That's what the Lord wants to build into each of our lives. The question is, Will you let Him?

Abraham, how did you do it?
Was your father-love so shallow
it meant nothing, or your trust so deep
you couldn't withhold even him?

It's hard to picture God
asking me to offer my son.
Tying the boy up.
Fending off his questions.
Calming him.
Then picking up the knife.
Poising it at his throat.

I mean, it't crazy.
It's plumb nuts, bonkers-wild,
dead in the head, lamebrain-mad
CRAZY!

What could I say to the judge?
"I was just doing what God told me to do!"
All the nuts plead that.

To top it all, this is in the Bible.
One of the greatest stories
in Hebrew history.
Preachers hold it up as the ultimate
object lesson.

Almost makes you think following God
requires total slavery—
or is it total trust?

Abraham, tell me your secret.
Show me the way.
I want to sink my faith deep
as faith can go.

2

Abraham:

"I CAN'T GIVE UP THAT"

At first Abraham was simply stunned. "Isaac? My son Isaac?" he mumbled under his breath.

As the afternoon wore on, he reviewed God's words a hundred times: "Take your son, your only son, whom you love, and go to the land of Moriah; and offer him there as a burnt offering."

For a hundred years Abraham and Sarah had lived without a son. Then the miracle happened. Abraham had watched Isaac grow. Even at his ancient age, he ran with the boy, poked him playfully in the ribs as they wrestled in the grass, and taught him to notch an arrow, fire it at a hanging apple or fig thirty yards away, and drop it at one shot. Fatherhood fit him like a Hittite sandal or a Jebusite cloak. Often he'd simply sit in the doorway of the tent and laugh as Isaac leaped with the dogs or bounced on a camel's back or coaxed a donkey with a load. He was proud and he was fulfilled. "An old man and full of days."

Yet, in a moment it would all be gone. A burnt offering. Isaac. His son. His only son. All he could see were the long years ahead. No grandchildren pawing his beard and climbing into his lap pleading for a story. No son edging into the tent and saying, "Father, I need your advice."

31

Abraham was tempted to argue with God, to shout "Why?" Even to shake his head and say, "No, I won't do it. Never."

All night he sat by the fire, tended the coals, gazed at his sleeping son. Sarah awakened twice, pulled a blanket over her shoulders, and ambled out. "What is wrong, lord? Can I bring you some refreshment?"

He had waved her away. "I must think, Sarah. Go back to sleep."

When the sun broke the horizon and gleamed across Abraham's hunched form, he jolted alert. He had dozed. But the brief sleep had dispelled none of his anxiety. His hand shook as he saddled his donkey, roused the young men, and finally touched Isaac's shoulder to awaken him.

Isaac rubbed his eyes and smiled. But Abraham turned away and said, "Get ready as quickly as possible. We must be off."

"What's the hurry?" Isaac asked. "It's only a sacrifice."

Abraham's throat tightened, but he said, "Please arise, my son. Sacrifice or not, we must obey God."

His own words almost seared his heart. "Must obey God." *But why?* he thought. Is there never a time for disagreement, for discussion even with God? Does He think nothing of human feelings?

In three days they reached the mountain. They left the young men behind and trudged on alone. Isaac carried the wood. Abraham held the torch for the fire. And in his bag, the knife.

As Abraham visualized the moment that would come all too soon, Isaac spoke. "But where's the lamb, Father? The sacrifice?"

Abraham's voice was low. "God will provide it, my son." As they drew closer to the top, his heart began to thunder.

It took only a few minutes to ask Isaac to submit to the bonds and lie on the altar. Then the boy asked the question Abraham had hoped he would never ask. "Why are we doing this, Father? Am I to die?"

Abraham looked deeply into his son's eyes. His mind scrabbled through ten planned statements. But he said, "I can't explain now, my son. Only trust me. You know I love you." His cheek twitched and he bit his lip. Isaac nodded and closed his eyes. Abraham poised the knife above Isaac's neck.

Momentarily he looked to heaven, uttered a silent prayer, and flexed his arm for the thrust.

Instantly a voice cried out, "Abraham! Abraham!" Abraham jumped. "I'm here, Lord." An angel appeared. "Do not touch the lad," he said, "for now I know that you fear God, since you have not withheld your only son from Me."

Abraham slumped, then turned as a noise alerted him to a ram caught in the thicket. He sacrificed it in Isaac's place.

Later, as they meandered down the mountain laughing and talking of this greatest of all experiences, Abraham recalled his words to Isaac.

Suddenly, he paused a moment and bowed before heaven, whispering, "Yes, Lord, I know You love me. I shall always trust You."

GOD WILL ASK FOR EVERYTHING

Think of it. God demanding that you sacrifice your son! Has God ever asked something similar from you? Maybe not something as dramatic. For each of us, the moment is different. Often it's more than just a moment. It's a whole lifetime of "turning over the keys of your kingdom." Yet there comes that single episode in the Christian walk when the Spirit speaks to us through His word, and we know God is asking, "Will you offer Me everything without reservation?"

You sputter, "Could it mean being a missionary?"

"Yes."

"Could it mean giving up my life savings?"

"Yes."

You sit in stunned silence for a minute. An hour. A day. A year. You even hope the question echoing inside of you will fizzle out. But it doesn't. Every time you go to church, every time you see a Bible, every time you meet a fellow Christian, the question echoes inside your heart like a train whistle. It will all come down to a dilemma: Do I obey God or do I run?

WHY GOD BRINGS US TO SUCH DECISIONS

Why does God provoke such decisions? Why does He ask us to sacrifice those things that rip at the core of our hearts? Understanding God's purposes behind such demands will help us obey His requirements—and to do so with joy.

TO SEE WHERE OUR HEARTS ARE

One reason comes directly out of Abraham's story. The moment he poised the knife to kill his son, the "angel of the LORD"—the Old Testament manifestation of Jesus Christ—appeared and said, "'Do not stretch out your hand against the lad . . . ; for now I know that you fear God, since you have not withheld your son, your only son, from Me'" (Genesis 22:12).

God wants to know whether we truly fear Him. He wants to know, "Will you obey me even when what I ask looks preposterous, costly, or painful?"

TO TEACH US TRUE WORSHIP

God also tests us so that we may experience true worship. Paul instructed the Romans to offer their bodies as "a living and holy sacrifice, acceptable to God, which is your spiritual service of worship" (Romans 12:1). Real worship involves sacrifice; anything less is lip service and pretense. God desires our untainted worship.

Forms of "worship" abound—meetings, singing, vibrant testimonies, powerful entertainments. We laugh. We cry. We pile on the compliments to the speaker and the chorus. But was there real sacrifice? Other than "giving up an evening," was there any evidence of people offering themselves? Often there is not. But when Abraham offered to God the one thing in his life that cost him everything, he truly worshiped. He knew God was worthy of his utmost obedience, and his sacrifice demonstrated the reality of his faith.

TO PROVE OUR FAITH TO THE WORLD

Some might question why God, who is omniscient, would initiate such a test if He already knew Abraham would obey. He knew Abraham's heart, it's true, but He wanted to prove before the world that Abraham had real faith.

In a sense making a confession of faith is a poker game. We think we have a winning hand, but God calls us. If we're bluffing, the test will show it. We'll cut and run in the cost of the play. Jesus talks about this testing of our faith in the Parable of the Soils. Those whose seed of faith was sown on thorny or shallow soil lost their faith when testing or temptation came. God called their bluff. But if we have true faith, we shine. We bear fruit. We persevere through the trial. In effect we lay down the cards and God is pleased, even though He knew all along. The process of testing is God's worldwide poker game that weeds out the bluffers from the faithful.

TO DEVELOP CHRISTLIKENESS

There's a fourth reason God takes us through testing: that we might become like Christ. How does He make us like Christ? By taking us down the same highways as Jesus— the pathway of obedience and suffering. Jesus blazed the trail; we follow in His steps—sometimes staggering, sometimes sprinting, but always with His Spirit.

HOW WE STAND WHEN GOD ASKS FOR EVERYTHING

In itself, an understanding of *why* God tests us does not always bring us comfort. It's similar to our response to the dentist who tells us why we need a root canal. What we want to know is, "How do I hang in there while he's drilling?" How then do we stand in the midst of this kind of test?

It's not easy. Satan's at our elbow shouting "Run!" The world snickers in our face, "Fool!" and our own flesh screeches under the weight, saying, "Think about yourself, your family, your career." Yet Abraham stood firm. The text reveals several principles to help us deal with such a test.

DON'T DEMAND AN EXPLANATION FROM GOD

The most incredible line in this whole story comes directly after God's terrible command. "So Abraham rose early in the morning and saddled his donkey" (Genesis 22:3). Undoubtedly Abraham had debated God's command the whole night. But come morning, his decision was made. Though he may still have been mystified and had no clear answers, he concluded, "Though I don't understand why, I'll obey anyway."

Have you ever come to that conclusion—"Forget the understanding; full obedience ahead"? We discussed in chapter one how Moses obeyed God despite his feelings. Here we see Abraham obeying God despite his lack of understanding. That's a primary principle: *Obey even when you don't understand what God is doing.*

God often commands people to carry out orders that defy human reason and experience: Adam couldn't eat the fruit of one tree; Noah built an ark on dry land in an age when there wasn't even rain; Joshua marched around Jericho. And the incident with Isaac was not the first time God had asked Abraham, without explanation, to do something unusual. When God first called him out of Ur, He simply said, "Go to a land I will show you." After that He promised Abraham a son through barren Sarah. Next God changed his name from Abram (Father) to Abraham (Father of nations)—and he hadn't had even one son through Sarah!

When we are asked to obey God simply because He asks us to, our faith is developed. After all, faith is believing God even when everyone else in the world screams, "No way! It's a lie! He's asking too much!" If we obeyed only when we understood, how would we ever accomplish anything? The essence of faith is "the conviction of things not seen" (Hebrews 11:1). God wants us to learn to trust Him implicitly. He wants us to believe whatever He says, even when what He says runs against reason like sandpaper on slate.

God, our heavenly Father, often relates to His children in the same way we as parents relate to our children. Let me explain. My wife and I are teaching Nicole, our two-year-old daughter, the meaning of "No" in relation to lamp wires. Every time we spot her running tests on those lines, we say "No!" and, if necessary, apply the palm treatment. We don't try to explain to her the nature of electricity. Can you imagine her demanding an explanation as to why such nasty orders are given?

God is da Vinci, Newton, and Einstein magnified to infinity. He knows the number of hairs on our heads. Neither atoms, earthquakes, cancer, the weather, or black holes mystify Him. Yet we, like one-year-olds, often demand to know why He's doing what He's doing to us, saying, "And don't get too technical. I have a headache!" Often He has to reply, "You can't understand. Just obey."

But suppose God had chosen to offer some explanation to Abraham. Besides the reason revealed by the angel—to confirm Abraham's faith—perhaps there were other reasons. God might have said, "Well, Abraham, your obedience this afternoon will affect a decision Isaac makes tonight in dealing with one of the younger men on the way home. In turn, the servant, when he gets home, will thank his wife for dinner instead of complaining. That in turn will cause her to be forgiving toward her son for slinging a stone at a camel and toppling a load of melons. Because of his mother's kind discipline throughout life, the boy will grow up to become a wise judge rather than a cruel overlord."

The Lord might go on to show how Abraham's obedience would influence everyday decisions in people's lives all through history. In that brief moment on the mountain, God not only saw Abraham and Isaac, but Martin Luther, John Calvin, Dwight Moody, you, and me. But how could God explain in detail how Abraham's actions would influence billions?

Similarly, how do we know what ultimate effects our obedience has on others? Or our sin? Only God sees the full ramifications of decisions which look to us to be isolated events. Thus God charges us to obey Him even when we don't understand. He's working the plan of the ages, not the whim of the moment.

Sometimes God does provide an explanation, though not always. When my wife and I looked over the bills we received from the hospital following the birth of our daughter, we were genuinely frightened. God has since provided the perspective and understanding we needed. At the time, though, He couldn't give us that perspective because intense pain and anxiety drowns out reason, logic, and theology no matter how hard we might try to hold on.

When my daughter received her diphtheria shot, she wailed and tried desperately to shove the doctor away. Valerie couldn't explain to Nicole why this was happening. But as Nicole cried and screamed, Valerie took her in her arms, kissed her, and hugged her tightly and lovingly. When God takes us through trials like Abraham's, He doesn't give us explanations; He takes us in His arms and gives us Himself.

REMIND YOURSELF OF WHO GOD IS

But one might reply, "I can see it in those situations, Mark. But what God was asking of Abraham was incredible. This was his son, his most precious possession." This brings us to a second principle: *Obey on the basis of what you already know about God.*

One reason Abraham acted so quickly on God's command was because he knew God and what He was like. He knew God was good, wise, kind, holy, and perfectly loving, with Abraham's best interests always in mind. He had learned those things through countless experiences with the Lord previous to this test. When Abraham went down into Egypt and lied about Sarah being his sister, God proved His faithfulness in protecting Abraham from his own stupidity. After that it was the problem with Lot's shepherds. Abraham gave Lot first choice of the land. When Lot took the best, Abraham might have despaired, thinking, *God's promise won't come true.* But again, God assured him with bold new promises. So when God asked Abraham to do something extremely painful and soul-rending, Abraham didn't flinch. He knew by now that God's thoughts aren't our thoughts, nor His ways our ways.

In the face of a tough test like this, we can ask ourselves, "What do I know of God from past experience—my own or those in Scripture?" Use that as the guide for your decisions, not some sudden impulse that says "Run! He'll ruin your life!"

Early in my Christian life the Lord convicted me about the foolishness of hitchhiking. About this same time I needed a ride home from college shortly before an Easter vacation. It was a trip of some 240 miles. I decided to pay the seven dollars for a ride home.

Shortly after we started the drive, I learned there were drugs in the car. Instantly the Spirit spoke to my heart and a terrific inner argument began in my mind. It seemed the Lord was telling me I had no business being in a car with illegal drugs. Though I'd often done this sort of thing as an unbeliever, I now knew it was wrong.

I battled with the Spirit, even offering to buy the drugs and fling them out the window. But the Lord kept returning to the thought that what I was doing was illegal, regardless of whether we were caught. We were in the middle of nowhere. "How," I kept asking, "will I get home if I can't hitchhike?" It seemed that the Lord reminded me, "Have I ever led you astray before?" I couldn't argue with that. I finally asked to get out. My friends argued with me, even offering to stay well below the speed limit. But I had to leave.

I got out. Not knowing what else to do, I turned and stuck out my thumb. The first car that came around the bend was a policeman! He picked me up and lectured me about the evils of hitchhiking, saying the fine would be forty dollars. Already I was thinking, *Here I had a ride home for seven dollars, Lord, and now I'm getting a forty dollar fine in addition to not having any other way home. Thanks a lot.*

But the Lord had other things in mind. When the policeman took me to a bus station, for some reason he didn't ticket me. When I found out the bus ticket cost fifteen dollars I decided to wait for a little while. Soon a couple of students walked in carrying Bibles. They began witnessing to people in the bus station. I reluctantly approached them and told them I was a new Christian. Immediately they invited me to stay the night at their school, saying their parents were coming up the next day and could give me a ride to a train station where I would be only a short train ride from home.

I was astounded. Not only did I end up having a fantastic time of fellowship with a group of zealous Christians, but my train fare was only three dollars. I ended up saving money! Once again, God had proven Himself faithful.

While you may not understand why God is asking you to give something up, you can look back to the ways He's been faithful in the past. That assures us that everything will turn out for the good.

DON'T EXPECT IT TO WORK OUT THE WAY YOU THINK

There's a tendency in all of us to become pessimistic. We tell ourselves, "What if this or that happens?" We're sure of the worst. But there's a another principle at work in Abraham's life that provides one more grain of hope. When Isaac asked where the lamb was, Abraham replied, "God will provide for Himself the lamb for the burnt offering" (Genesis 22:8). Had Abraham really been willing to go through with the sacrifice of his son? Yes. But he knew something else about God: *God's ways are unpredictable.* Things will usually turn out different from and better than we think.

Abraham knew that walking with God was an adventure. He could never anticipate the marvels and wonders God would bring his way. Hebrews tells us Abraham believed God could raise the dead. So even if Isaac was sacrificed, Abraham knew God could bring his son back to life. Abraham didn't know what God would do, but he did know it would work out for the best.

MY TEST

Years ago, God demanded something from me that looked like everything. I was working as a short-order chef in a ski lodge in Vermont. One week I began to feel a bit depressed and thought something was wrong. I went down to the local "Chapel of the Snows" and began praying. Suddenly it was in my mind that God wanted me to become a minister. Though I had often thought about it and though some people even suggested it after my conversion, I had written off the idea. I didn't know how to do anything ministers did—I was terrified of public speaking; I knew nothing about counseling; I had never led anyone to Christ. More importantly to me, the only ministers I had known in my childhood were lackluster, dull men who bored me every Sunday. I simply didn't want to be identified with them, though as a new Christian I had heard and profited from many men of God.

I tried to push the idea out of my mind. It was a ploy of Satan. It was a psychological impression. It was my nervous system gone berserk. But God wouldn't let go. I argued, wept, screamed, pleaded. But finally I gave in, saying, "Okay, Lord, I'll be a minister. But You have to show me I can speak in public, and lead people to Christ, and be a counselor. Furthermore, You'll have to convince me the ministry can become my life's greatest source of joy." I didn't think even God could do that.

But then He began ticking off those items. First He dealt with my fear of public speaking. One evening later that week, I was studying my Bible in the sitting room of the lodge restaurant. A man sauntered up to me, noted my Bible, and said, "Are you a Jesus freak?"

I replied, "Well, in a way." I didn't want to press it.

But he did. He asked, "What happened to you? I've heard about so many of these people changing the direction of their lives." I began giving my testimony. After all, it was only one on one. A minute after I began, some friends of his wandered in and he called them over. "Listen to this guy!" he said. More guests ambled in and joined the crowd. Soon fifteen or twenty people were listening to me. I was not afraid; in fact I was enjoying it. When it was over I marveled: "That wasn't so bad, Lord."

The next event on God's agenda was with a co-worker who had cursed me, threatened me with a knife, and told me to stop telling her present boyfriend premarital sex was wrong (they were living together). One day a previous boyfriend of hers—one who used to beat her—showed up, and she was terrified. As we worked together making sandwiches, she asked me about Jesus. I began giving my testimony and sharing verses. After an hour's discussion, I asked her, "Do you want to become a Christian?" She replied, "I just did while you were talking! I asked the Lord to come into my life." I was stunned.

Afterward I was sitting in our foyer reading a book about Satan. A woman guest at the lodge sat down opposite me. Suddenly she burst into tears, saying, "Are you a Christian?" I nodded and she poured out a terrible story of a son who had gotten involved in the occult and ended up a schizophrenic. She didn't know what to do. Could I help?

Suddenly Proverbs 3:5-6 popped into my head. I turned to it, began explaining the passage, and told her how the Lord had helped me with problems through that text. At the end she remarked, "You know, you ought to be a counselor. You're really good!" I was astonished. I had been sure God couldn't answer any of those requests. But after seeing what happened in that short month after our conversation in the chapel, I didn't want to be anything but a minister! It couldn't be anything less than the key to the greatest joy and fulfillment in my life.

WHEN IT HAPPENS TO YOU

What about you? Has God confronted you with a request that seems to demand your very lifeblood, something so precious you feel you can't possibly give it up to Him?

There are many things you can do about it: Run. Fight. Ignore it. Rationalize it away. Even pretend to give in, thinking that if you just offer it verbally God won't care what's in your heart.

Instead, why not say Yes. Tell Him, "I know You're trustworthy and have always proved faithful before. Even though I don't understand, I know I love You. More importantly, I know You love me."

It could be the beginning of something so wonderful you'll be praising Jesus forever after that He brought you to that point.

I tend to picture this
barrel-chested fellow
with a huge beard,
wild eyes, shiny white teeth.
Very serious.
Big voice. When he spoke
people listened, even
if they didn't believe.
The kind of person people talk about
in whispers.
Tough. Hammered a nail
with one whack.
No one like him before or since.
God's man in an age
when everyone else loved Satan.
Stood where everyone else slid.

But who knows? Maybe
he was this spindly little fellow
with a squeaky voice
who simply loved God.
Maybe when he drove nails
he missed more times than he hit.
Maybe his boat floated only
because God was in it.
Maybe as he stood alone
his knees clacked together.

Who knows? Maybe
he was a guy
not a whole lot different from you
_or me._

3

Noah:

"THERE'S NOBODY ELSE BUT ME"

Everyone in the office liked her. Several of the men began asking her out. A few times she consented without knowing their spiritual convictions. When they found out she didn't believe in premarital sex, things got hot. "It's reserved only for marriage," she told them when they pressed their case. The other girls in the office repeatedly taunted her about it, saying, "You ought to grow up." And, "You're missing so much." One coworker brought in a special pen with graphic sexual design.

When she refused to succumb to these manipulations, she became the office joke. Some said they ought to stuff her and send her to the Smithsonian as "The Last American Virgin." Several of the men even considered it their duty to bring her up to par sexually and began baiting her.

Her boss noted a rash she had on her hand and said, "What's that—herpes?" When she continued to decline his offers to take her with him on weekend business excursions, he began writing condemning memos pronouncing her as incompetent, haughty, and inflexible. She finally decided to resign and seek work elsewhere.

But the scars remain.

ALL OF US WILL STAND ALONE SOMETIME

One of faith's most difficult challenges is standing alone. All of us are challenged to stand alone at one point or another.

The teen who won't smoke marijuana while his friends mock him.

The housewife whose bridge group argues with her on the issue of submission to her husband.

The salesman who refuses to deceive a customer, though the sale would be impossible otherwise.

The godly elder whose church is slipping into liberalism.

Standing for Christ, truth, and holiness in such situations isn't easy. While we're not in peril for our lives, our egos can easily be shaken by the rejection, anger, mockery, and even hatred that is leveled at us. We know God will never desert us nor forsake us, but sometimes flesh-and-blood humans seething in our face seem a lot bigger than God at that moment. Often we feel as though God has disappeared entirely, leaving us to face His enemies alone. Where can we find help when the room goes silent, the faces turn in our direction, the eyes glare, and we suddenly realize no one's on our side?

Nearly every godly saint in Scripture stood alone at some point in their lives—Abraham during the rescue of Lot, David when King Saul pursued him relentlessly, Jeremiah, Isaiah, Habakkuk, Nehemiah, and many others. One who stands out above them all is Noah. He stood alone as perhaps no one else has before or since. He lived in an age so wicked, God decided to destroy everything. Every motive was corrupt, every plan perverted. Man had reached his lowest point as a race. Yet God was gracious. His eyes moved throughout the earth and lit upon a single holy man: Noah—a lily thriving by a cesspool.

God spoke to Noah and gave him a job: Build a giant ship capable of keeping a multitude of animals and people safe while a flood eliminated every other trace of life.

THE CIRCUMSTANCES OF STANDING ALONE

Noah's situation not only provides insight into our own circumstances; but it can also infuse us with hope. If Noah did it then, we can do it now.

Consider just what he was up against. First, there was the task itself. This ark was to be 450 feet long—as large as a modern pleasure ship. No one had ever built such a thing. Noah had to use primitive tools and craftsmanship. There would be no second chance. Noah must have gazed many times on his backyard wonder and thought, *It'll never float. We'll go down like a rock!*

Second, there were questions, doubts. Noah battled with the same issues any person battles in such an undertaking. Can I do it right? Why am I the chosen one? What if I fail? There were probably days when Noah marched into his office, fell down on his knees, and cried, "God, help! The workers are calling in sick. My own family is dead tired. And we can't find a tree big enough for the keel. Can't we do it some other way?" He probably asked himself, *Is God really going to destroy the whole world? Is it that bad?* Noah might even have questioned his own sanity. *Have I deluded myself? Is all this stuff about God just a figment of my imagination?*

Third, there was the strange normalcy of his times. Jesus said that the last days will be just like the days of Noah. Everyone will be "eating and drinking, marrying and giving in marriage" (Matthew 24:37). When things appear normal, we tend to slack off, slow down, and forget the urgency of our situation.

Fourth, there was the ridicule. What happened when the local real estate agents were showing off their properties? They probably mentioned Noah. "Basically, we've got a nice community. But we do have this one nut." Noah preached to the people who came by gawking and mocking. Undoubtedly, many joked about him, imitated him, even hated him.

Fifth, there was the pain of knowing the truth. Though the people mocked, Noah still knew the flood would come. Some of these people were friends and neighbors. If they didn't repent, they would perish. Perhaps as Noah assured them of the coming judgment, one said, "Oh, it's never that bad, Noah." Others felt sorry for him. "He used to be a pretty sound fellow, but I don't know what's happened to him." Still others tried to talk him out of it. "You're a good businessman, Noah. Why waste your time on this nonsense?" But the worst were those who agreed: "Yes, I suppose I ought to change my ways. I'll think about it. You've made a lot of sense."

Noah hoped and preached, preached and prayed—yet no one believed. Only his wife, his sons, and their wives stood with him. One of the greatest trials in standing alone is the ache you feel when people you love reject Christ. Something within us dies when a relative or friend shrugs off the gospel and says, "That's okay for you. But I have another way."

Sixth, there was the wear and tear of it all. It's easy to stick with something for a week or two. But Noah pounded nails, preached his simple messages, and toted lumber for over a century. Adoniram Judson, missionary to Burma, labored for eight years before he saw a single convert. William Wilberforce debated the slavery issue for decades in England's Parliament before anyone listened.

Obviously, Noah's situation was far more drastic than most of us can ever know. But when we must stand alone, when the torch is pressed to our skin, no one else will matter but us.

HELPS FOR SURVIVAL

The narrative in Genesis 6-9 provides keen insights for how we can stand alone in this world. While such circumstances are difficult, they're not impossible—and rewards are there, too.

LEARN TO RELY ON GOD'S GRACE

The first indicator of Noah's source of strength is in Genesis 6:8—"But Noah found favor in the eyes of the LORD."

The words translated "found favor" could go two ways. One interpretation is that God looked down from heaven, spotted Noah, and determined to give him unsolicited help and friendship. A second idea is that Noah himself turned to God for help. Perhaps the best way is a combination of the two. God's favor couldn't be earned and was offered on God's initiative. But Noah also sought it; he called on God for help in time of trouble.

This is the essence of the Christian life. "Apart from Me you can do nothing," Jesus said (John 15:5). No hope, no talent, no plan, no desire will ever succeed apart from Jesus' involvement and control.

For many of us the truth of God's grace is not new. We've heard the message of grace from countless authors and teachers. And yet we remain mystified. The popular definition of "unmerited favor" doesn't strike home. We are left asking, What is grace?

Try this thought. God's grace is His willingness to give us any divine resource we need to live a God-honoring life. It's given not on the basis of our worthiness, but because of His love. What are the divine resources available to us? Read about them in such passages as Galatians 5:22-23 (the fruit of the Spirit), 1 Corinthians 13 (the love chapter), Ephesians 1—3 (our position in Christ), and Romans 1—8 (all God has done in saving and sanctifying us).

Peter captured a potent idea when he said, "His divine power has granted to us everything pertaining to life and godliness" (2 Peter 1:3). That's the vision. God has given us *everything* for life and godliness. If we need wisdom, we call to Him (James 1:5-6). Endurance? He is able to supply it (2 Corinthians 12:9-10). Opportunities to serve Him? He has planned them all in advance (Ephesians 2:10). Faith, hope, or love? Look at Ephesians 3:16-21. God is "able to do exceeding abundantly beyond all that we ask or think."

Are you seeking God's grace in all circumstances of life? When you stand alone, is your first response to pray and ask God for His help? Or is it to plough ahead on instinct or common sense? Your answer will indicate why you stand or fall when you stand alone.

God gives us grace when we ask Him for it. As the author of the letter to the Hebrews said, "Let us therefore draw near with confidence to the throne of grace, that we may receive mercy and may find grace to help in time of need" (Hebrew 4:16). There's no reason to conjure up all kinds of complicated steps and processes. Ask.

I find that the Lord answers such requests in a multitude of ways—from instantaneous insights to labyrinthine processes of study worked out over years. There is no formula. But He has committed Himself to meeting our needs (Philippians 4:19), which includes providing the resources necessary to stand firm.

DISCOVER THE POWER OF A RIGHTEOUS AND BLAMELESS LIFE

The second indicator of Noah's source of strength comes from Genesis 6:9—"Noah was a righteous man, blameless in his time." "Righteous" pictures Noah's standing before other people. It means to "conform to a standard, to meet the requirements of what is right and just." "Blameless" identifies his standing before God. His record was unblotched. This doesn't mean Noah was sinless; rather, he conformed to the revelation and truth God had given him, while seeking God's grace and forgiveness when he made mistakes. He had cast himself on God's mercy. Because he was righteous, no man could accuse him of wrongdoing. Noah could preach the truth without flinching and live out his faith with confidence.

Peter gives the real power of this in a poignant passage.

> Who is there to harm you if you prove zealous for what is good? But even if you

should suffer for the sake of righteousness, you are blessed. And do not fear
their intimidation, and do not be troubled,
but sanctify Christ as Lord in your hearts,
always being ready to make a defense to
everyone who asks you to give an account
for the hope that is in you, yet with gen-
tleness and reverence; and keep a good
conscience so that in the thing in which
you are slandered, those who revile your
good behavior in Christ may be put to
shame. (1 Peter 3:13-16)

Note Peter's conclusions about righteous living. First, you can live in the world without fear of harm. No one will be out to get you. Second, if you are persecuted, it's actually a blessing. It will only give you a chance to speak up for the truth. Third, if you make a mistake, make it right as soon as possible. That way no one will have any justifiable reason to accuse you.

But Noah's blamelessness gave him a second boost. He knew God was on his side. He could depend on God to come through in the clutch.

When we sin, we not only destroy our testimony in the world, but also our fellowship with God. We can't be sure He'll support us because He moves from deliverer to disci-plinarian. Remember what happened to Joshua after the triumph at Jericho? The people attacked Ai. But they were soundly defeated because Achan had taken some articles the Lord had put under the ban. One man's sin led to defeat for the whole nation. Can we think that God will support us when we willfully disobey Him?

Ask yourself: "Does anyone have anything against me?" If so, make it right. Then, "Have I done anything to offend God?" If nothing comes to mind after prayer, there's no need for anxiety. But if there is real guilt and you see sin, confess it. Straighten it out. You can't stand alone with ex-cess baggage on your shoulders.

START PRACTICING A CLOSE DAILY WALK
WITH THE LORD

Genesis 6:9 also reveals the third essential element for standing alone: "Noah walked with God." In all of history, Enoch is the only other person who was said to have "walked with God." Interestingly enough, he was Noah's great-grandfather. Though Noah could never have known him personally (according to the chronologies of Genesis), he must have heard much about this godly man. In addition, Noah's father, Lamech, was a righteous man. He even predicted that Noah would be the one to preserve the race (Genesis 5:29). Clearly, Noah had access to the wisest men of his age when it came to walking with God.

Walking with God is another of those word pictures in the Bible that often go over our heads. Paul used the image in describing the Christian life. "But I say, walk by the Spirit, and you will not carry out the desire of the flesh" (Galatians 5:16). "We walk by faith, not by sight" (2 Corinthians 5:7). "Walk in a manner worthy of the Lord" (Colossians 1:10). "Walk as children of light" (Ephesians 5:8). Obviously, the idea of walking is an important analogy. It's easy to picture, but how does it work out in practical living?

Walking is a slow, steady movement toward a goal. The person who walks with God knows where he's going. He doesn't run or even jog. He just makes progress in the right direction. It's also an activity for which a man is perfectly suited. Walking is the most natural way for people to get anywhere. It doesn't require massive effort. Just endurance. In addition, it's something we learn and develop as we grow. A baby stands, wobbles, crashes, cries. Eventually, he ventures tiny steps while holding onto a table. Then he tries it without the props. Soon he's making beelines across the living room. Ultimately he no longer thinks about it. He just does it.

I've often pictured walking with God as being similar to a hike with a close friend or spouse. As we walk along, we comment to one another about things we observe. We ask questions—"Isn't that pretty?" "What do you think of this?"—and listen to the answers. For a while we may discuss some political, theological or moral issue. We might argue or debate. We may discuss a matter that troubles us, and ask for advice. For a moment we may simply stop together and silently enjoy a sunset.

In such a situation, there are no rules. We don't stop and say, "Now at the beginning of our hike I have reserved five minutes where you can talk to me. So start right now." No, it's give and take, speak and listen, embrace and move apart. It's a love relationship. We simply relish one another's presence.

That's walking with God. It's not a mechanical keeping of a series of rules. It's much like the give and take of a joyous, intimate marriage, a friendly business relationship, or a longtime friendship, even though it's creature to Creator.

That's what Noah had. God was his closest friend. As Noah drove nails into the ark, he discussed the great questions he had. As he gazed at night at the stars of heaven, he praised and thanked God. As he hurried about buying timber and hiring workers, he asked God for direction. When his family sat down to dinner, they shared what they had learned from the Lord that day.

Fellowship with God is what kept Noah strong when everything else was shaky. When people shrieked and laughed at him, he knew God was right there at his side. When he felt depressed, he shared his thoughts with his Lord, and God comforted him. That's the kind of walk Jesus wants with us.

LEARN TO OBEY EVEN UNTO DEATH

Genesis 6:22 and 7:5 reveal a fourth characteristic of this man who stood alone so firmly: "Thus Noah did; according to all that God had commanded him, so he did." Here was a man given a task so huge that any hesitation on his part would have been fully understandable. Yet he did exactly as God commanded him. No arguing. No trying to tell God a better way. Just humble obedience.

Moses obeyed despite his feelings, and Abraham obeyed even when he didn't understand, but Noah's obedience is another brand—what I'd call routine faithfulness, just obeying God in the daily routine of life. That's what Noah had to do.

Some time ago I was involved in a group of ministers who met to discuss theology, our work, and the usual things. On one occasion, I shared something God had been teaching me from 1 Timothy. I said, "I'm always wanting to do my thing in the ministry—trying to come up with some way to make the church grow, get things moving. But recently I read a verse in 1 Timothy in which Paul told his disciple—"'Until I come, devote yourself to the public reading of scripture, to preaching and to teaching'" (4:13).

I said, "You know, I've always thought of the reading of the Scripture from the pulpit as a kind of necessary, though dry, part of the service. Preaching, too, was important, but not as much as counseling and 'making people feel good in church.'

"But I've been learning that the things I ought to major on are right here in Timothy—reading Scripture, preaching, and teaching. I've decided that whatever the Bible says, I'm going to do. No arguing. No trying my own way. Just plough ahead with it. I'm excited about it."

I glanced around at the group of men enthusiastically. I thought they'd say, "Hey, you're really starting to see the light, brother." Or, "Tell me more." Instead, one of them said rather abruptly, "What you're talking about sounds like bibliolatry to me. You can't put the Bible above Jesus. You've got to get away from all this literalism." We turned to other subjects.

Suddenly I realized again that obeying God 'literally' according to His word is what standing alone is all about. That was what Noah did. Though the world went on without a sign of destruction, though the idea of a flood seemed preposterous, he obeyed. When people mocked him and laughed, it might have been difficult. But Noah told himself, "I won't believe them. I'll obey God." The destruction was still a hundred years away, but Noah kept banging in those nails. His sons wanted to make the ark shorter, but Noah held firm. "We're doing everything God said. Three hundred cubits." When his wife told him she couldn't stand the smell and wanted to jump out, Noah replied, "Wait on the Lord. He's been faithful so far, hasn't He?"

That's standing alone—sticking with the job God gave you no matter who or how many are against you.

What about you? Is that how you obey Him—doing exactly as His word prescribes? Or do you add your own variations, make the changes you think are necessary, apply it only when you feel like it?

THE END OF STANDING ALONE

Standing alone isn't necessarily synonymous with being lonely. Neither is it without its rewards. After the ark was built, the flood came and the world was destroyed, but Noah and his family were preserved. When they finally embarked into that new world, the first thing Noah did was worship. He prepared sacrifices of every clean animal and bird. God was pleased.

That's what happens when we stand alone: We worship God and He is pleased.

Can you think of a better conclusion?

A child. A baby.
That was all you wanted.

It started a hushed hope
at eighteen.

At twenty, a promise
without possibility of breech.

At twenty-two, a prayer cry
each night before bed, pleadings
with your husband.

At twenty-five, the fingers would bunch
into hard gnarls, the throat became tight,
the words within were like hot bricks
thudding into dirt.

By thirty, a rage,
and a grim despair. The eyes red
for days, the lips bitten.
Long hours spent staring across the fields,
swallowing at the sounds of children
singing, running, skipping.

Now at thirty-five, you form your last plan.
You walk into the temple, your head bent.
You wait long anquished minutes, breathing
shallow, fast.
Then you tell Him you will give Him the boy
at three, if only He will
give you a son.
A son. A son.
That's all.
The fruit of your womb.
The treasure of the heart.
Just one.
You weep as you pray.

For weeks after, each morning you listen
to the sounds of your body.
You touch your stomach and hope. Nothing.
You despair. The next day you hope again.

Then one day you know.
The joy surges through you
like spring water from winter mountains.
You bow. You worship. You weep.
You remember. Every day forever
you give thanks and love Your God.

4

Hannah:

"WHY WON'T YOU BLESS ME?"

Peninnah stood in the doorway and shouted at Hannah as she huddled on her bed. "It's because you have offended Jehovah. That's why you have no children. You'll never have children." She turned and stalked toward the door where her own children stood, wide-eyed but grinning.

Once more she turned. "And I'll have more children!" Hannah didn't move. "Then Elkanah will love me and he will hate you. Because you are childless." Peninnah's words rose in pitch. "Do you hear me? Barren!"

Hannah crumpled into a ball, rolled onto her side and faced the wall. She wished there would be peace. More, she wished she could have just one child—a son, a daughter. Just one.

When Elkanah came in from working in his fields, Peninnah displayed none of the anger she had shown earlier. He stooped by the fire where Hannah cooked, and he caressed her cheek. "My favorite!" he said. "You always cook my favorite on the Sabbath."

"Everything I cook you call your favorite," she said. "You're just easy to please."

He laughed. "It's all perfect," he said. "My two wives are the best any man could ask for."

He smiled at Hannah, then Peninnah.

"This year I will make a special sacrifice—one for my wife with many children and one for my wife with none." When Hannah's cheek flinched, he added, "But soon to have many as well."

Hannah bit her lip but didn't look up.

Elkanah cupped her chin with his hand and turned her face toward him. "You're not sad again?" he said, watching her eyes.

She shook her head quickly.

"Hannah, you must not fret about this. Jehovah will reward you. Wait. Be patient. You will have a child."

Hannah glimpsed into her husband's eyes. She knew he meant well. But she was thirty-two years old.

Two months later the family went up to Shiloh to offer the yearly sacrifices. As always Elkanah gave special offerings for everyone and a double portion for Hannah.

But that evening Hannah could not even cook supper. She lay on her bed weeping. Elkanah sat beside her stroking her hair and murmuring kind words. "My wife, am I not better to you than ten sons? Even if you never have a child, you have me. Our love will be greater than a hundred children."

Later Hannah went up to the temple to pray. Eli, the priest, sat by the doorpost and nodded as she went in, but said nothing. When she had been there nearly an hour, he walked in and sat a few paces behind her. The hour had been difficult. Sweat gleamed on her forehead in the firelight. She had promised God that if He gave her a son, she would give Him the child as a Nazirite. She murmured and sniffled quietly.

Eli thought she was drunk. He jumped up and said to her, "How can you come into God's house like this?"

Hannah shook and looked up.

"Put away your wine," he said harshly. "Don't come here drunk. It's blasphemous."

Hannah turned and bowed before him. "No, my lord, I'm not drunk. I've been praying to Jehovah. I've come only because of a great sorrow."

Eli's face softened. "Forgive my mistake." He touched her shoulder. "Go in peace. May the Lord grant your request."

Hannah's lips flickered a weak smile.

When she returned to the house where the family was staying, something within her seemed to glow and bounce. For the first time she felt a great confidence. *Even if I have no child,* she thought, *God is with me.*

When they returned to Ramah, Elkanah noted the change. "See, God has given you His joy. You don't need sons. You only need us."

As always, Peninnah was vengeful and cutting when she and Hannah were alone. "So you think you'll have a son this season next year?"

Hannah sighed. "I'm not sure. But my time of pain is over. I know God will do as is fitting."

"Ha!" Peninnah dropped the bucket in the well to draw water. "In six months you'll be weeping as never before."

Less than three months after their visit to Shiloh, Hannah was with child. She told Elkanah one evening as they sat under a fig tree. His excitement was instantaneous.

But after he had laughed and given a boisterous shout to God, she told him, "This son will be a Nazirite. I vowed to give him back to the Lord."

Elkanah became quiet and sat down, surveying her face. "You're sure it's a son?"

Hannah nodded.

Elkanah leaned back against the fig tree. "This will not give you pain—when you offer him to Eli for the temple work?"

Tears formed in Hannah's eyes. "I do not say that. But it is what I must do. I made a vow." Elkanah watched her eyes brim with tears. "You have done a bold thing. A good thing. Much will come of it."

Hannah smiled weakly. "I hope so. I believe so. I am very happy."

WANTING A BLESSING—AND NOT GETTING IT

All through the church there are Christians who, like Hannah, have lived with sorrow. They're not necessarily poor. They don't lack health or friends or pleasure. But there is something—perhaps just one thing—that they yearn for. It's a blessing they can never obtain by their wits, schemes, perseverance, or charm. Only God can grant it. Nevertheless, for some reason God refuses to answer Yes.

Though they pray and ask others to pray, though they try various tricks, listen to tapes constantly, read books, and even slip into manipulation and threats on occasion, nothing changes.

I think of Judy. A vivacious, kind woman. She sings, dances, organizes special events at church that all enjoy. She's attractive and interesting. She has an excellent career, but she wants a husband. She is approaching her late thirties and has not found that one man she feels would be right for her. She's struggled with depression, anger, frustration, and simply learning to wait. She's even "given it over to the Lord." It's easy for people to tell her "He'll come along" or "Look at it as a blessing." But I also have known that loneliness—it's an ache.

I think, too, of Doug. Converted several years ago, he is zealous, exuberant, excited about Jesus. But the shrill cry of his heart is, "Lord, bring my family to Jesus. Don't let them perish." His father is old. His mother is embedded in ritualistic Catholicism. There isn't much time left, but God seems not even to have moved, let alone converted.

I think of others. Chuck—out of work and no job in sight. Don and Mary—strong Christians, but their teenage children reject Christ and the faith. Brenda—her alcoholic husband shows no interest in the gospel, Jesus, or even love.

And I think of Hannah, the woman "of a sorrowful spirit." She knew well what it was to cry for God's blessing and to watch her prayers crash to the ground in resounding No's from heaven.

Can you identify?

If so, you can probably recall the variety of reactions you receive when trying to explain to others your feelings. Some are sympathetic but offer lame and even offensive advice like, "Just keep praying, God will come through," or, "Have you searched your heart to see if you've sinned in any way?" Searched your heart? You've dissected, flayed, chewed, and pounded it, trying to shake out that hidden sin you're so sure must be keeping God from blessing you.

Others accuse, much like Job's counselors. They don't *suggest* you might have sinned—they're certain you have! "You need to get right with God," they say.

Others don't understand why you're troubled. They don't wonder if you've sinned, they just wonder what your problem is. "What's the big deal? I wouldn't sweat that kind of thing."

Still others don't know what to say. You want to talk about it, you *need* to talk about it, but they put you off: "Don't worry, it'll work out," or a hurried "Well I've got to go, I'll be praying for you."

Beyond the problems with the reactions of others are your own feelings. Your emotions can trample you as they twist and spin within. The text says Hannah wouldn't eat, and wept continually.

Anger can sear your heart as you crash at the end of the week when you were so sure the answer would come. During a period of illness I pleaded for healing daily, but the pain always returned in jackhammer jolts of reality. I'd often cry to God, "Why are you doing this to me? Why won't you bless?" The answer didn't come for more than two years.

After the anger comes the feeling of rejection. You end up staring into space. *God's forsaken me. He doesn't care. He won't hear my prayers.*

In the midst of it, Scripture often doesn't help. You read God's word like a starving man grasping at grains of rice. You look for that one verse, that single sentence of assurance, that personal message from God—but it escapes you. You feel as though God has vanished.

Yet you're obsessed with one desire. You can't shake it. You tell yourself, "What's it matter? It's only a little thing"—but it doesn't work. This is the only thing that matters.

Hannah's desire for a child built in her mind over the years to a gigantic crescendo. As she aged, she became deeply depressed. While some women would have gritted their teeth and plodded on, Hannah was ready to give up. The question seemed to screech through her mind daily: "Will I die having never brought a child into the world?" For her, life wasn't worth living if she couldn't become a mother.

Indeed, to an Israelite woman motherhood was the epitome of personhood. In our day of liberation and career-orientation, we find it difficult to understand. But to God's people, barrenness was a sign of God's curse. Sarah, Rebekah, and Rachel, the mothers of the fathers of all Israelites, and Elizabeth, the mother of John the Baptist, were all barren for a period in their lives. Their pain was great. Rachel told Jacob, "Give me children, or I die" (Genesis 30:1). And when Elizabeth became pregnant with John, she told her husband, "God has taken away my disgrace" (Luke 1:35).

Reading about someone who went through a period without a specific blessing is one thing, but to be going through such a period yourself is another. Insight into why a problem occurs can provide hope and understanding to those living through a period of blessinglessness. If we can grasp why God sometimes doesn't bless a saint, we can endure. What then do we see God doing in Hannah's life while her blessing was delayed?

THE BYPRODUCTS OF WITHHELD BLESSINGS

When we approach a subject like this, it's always wise to ask what God's goals are for our lives. It's easy to confuse our desire for present happiness with God's will. We think because Jesus said, "I came that they might have life and have it abundantly" (John 10:10) that all bad things should be eliminated from our lives. But God's plan is to make us holy first, then happy. Only holiness produces genuine happiness. Ironically, the road to true holiness contains many unhappy byways.

DEVELOPS OUR HOLINESS

This brings us to a first principle about why God delays His blessing: *God knows about our desires but sometimes delays fulfilling them to train us in holy life.* God was more concerned about making Hannah a woman *of* God than making her a mother *for* God. Becoming a mother isn't difficult, but turning mothers into the likeness of Jesus takes work.

Scripture teaches that God is sovereign. Paul tells us in Ephesians 1:11 that He "works all things after the counsel of His will." He is Lord of all. Nothing that comes to pass surprises Him, catches Him off guard, or stumps Him. He planned it all from beginning to end. Nothing escapes His scrutiny and control. He's in charge. I believe God not only was aware and concerned about Hannah's problem, but in His perfect wisdom had also planned it this way for His own purpose—the development of holiness in her life.

We tend to rebel against this truth. "You mean God made her barren?" "You mean He put her through all that pain?" "You mean God is the cause of all this trouble?" Not the cause, but yes, it was part of His plan. To develop character in Hannah, God orchestrated the events of her life toward that end. To bring about true godlikeness in her life, He withheld the blessing.

Look at the byproducts of Hannah's time of trial: patience, endurance, a fervent prayer life, intimate knowledge of God, a passion for holiness. Would these things have come apart from her pain? To produce a Samuel, God first had to produce a Hannah.

As we undergo trials, Christians sometimes refer to this idea when they tell us, "God is trying to teach you something." At the funeral of a four-week-old child, I listened to a pastor say that God was "trying to teach us to trust Him." I was outraged. Did God have to kill a baby to teach a lesson? Are the trials of life merely to get information into our heads?

That notion is a subtle trap. When I have sought a certain blessing from God and gone through dry, barren periods of pain, I've often prayed, "What lesson are You trying to teach me, Lord? Then just teach it to me and let's get on with the show!" We tend to think God is trying to get some principle into our heads and that's it. But there's much more. If He simply wanted us to know facts and maxims, He'd jam a book into our hands and say, "Memorize it. When you're done, you'll be just like Me!" But is that all He is—a repository of knowledge?

No, he wants to transform us from sinners into the likeness of Jesus—not just "reasonable facsimiles thereof," not even reproductions, but sublime portraits in technicolor and panavision. That takes much more than book learning. What is required is a total life transformation. When we enter eternity, He wants all creation to look at us and remark, "That's what God is like!" He's planned every event of this life, every choice we face, every force brought to bear upon our body, soul, and spirit, as a means of shaping us into that likeness.

This may cause some Christians to cry, "Does this mean we have no freedom?" Of course not. That's part of being like God—being free. The more we become like Him, the more free we actually become.

Imagine a colony of rabbits who have a strange desire to fly. Most of them are killed in the process of trying, while the survivors sit about on their haunches and discuss their predicament.

Then along comes a special rabbit who explains to them that they were never meant to fly, but rather to run. Some of the rabbits scoff at him. But others listen, and the special rabbit shows these teachable ones how to run along mudpaths, down winding roads, across superhighways, through forests, and so on. They become the greatest runners in creation.

Which group of rabbits would you say is free? The rabbits trying to fly are doing their own thing. No one is lording it over them. But are they free? The other rabbits submit to the special rabbit. They believe in him. They obey him. And he enables them to become the most magnificent rabbits in creation. Does their submission mean they're not free?

While we are sinners, living ungodly, disobedient lives, we're like those rabbits trying to fly. We're not being what we were meant to be. But when we become Christians and submit to Christ, He teaches, empowers, and shapes us to become what we were meant to be all along: images of God, free in the power of the Spirit.

When we submit ourselves to God recognizing that He is sovereign and wise and has our highest good not only in heart but in plan, we can joyfully follow the path He has laid, giving thanks and praising Him. So when we seek His blessing and it doesn't come, we should "consider it all joy . . . knowing that the testing of your faith produces endurance " (James 1:2-3).

TEACHES US TO RELY ON THE CHURCH

The crushing disappointment we feel when we go without a particular blessing often *forces us to turn to other believers for support and encouragement.* In Hannah's case, God sent her at least one understanding friend: her husband, Elkanah. He sought to comfort her, encourage her, meet her needs. Though he could not crawl inside her body and experience her pain, he was both sympathetic and practical. He offered special sacrifices at the temple. When she tumbled into a quagmire of self-pity, he held her and assured her.

One of the things I most appreciate about Jesus is that He doesn't expect us to act like nonhumans. When God created Adam, He didn't turn into a egotistical lout and re-mark, "Well, Adam, now it's you and Me. You have all you need right here." No, He said, "It's not good for the man to be alone." Adam needed someone like himself. It's a bit like the little fellow who was afraid of the dark. His father told him when he cried from his bedroom, "God's up there with you, son." The boy replied, "I know. But I need someone with skin on." We all need someone with skin on now and then.

Praying doesn't bring a tangible expression of God's love. Sometimes reading and memorizing God's word isn't enough. Singing a hymn in the dark doesn't do it either. We need the warmth of the church, God's people, their words, their notes, their gifts.

We should never discount the power of the church in a crisis. We should not shirk their advice or shoulder off their attempts at friendship. Jesus says that we're all part of His body. That means we belong to and need one another. No one going through a period of blessinglessness should try to stand alone. Paul said, "Bear one another's burdens, and thus fulfill the law of Christ" (Galatians 6:2). The blow of bereftness is softened by the fellowship of saints who care for and love one another.

TEACHES US PERSISTENCE

Hannah's experience brought out a third truth about why God delays his blessing. *Wanting a blessing teaches us to persist.* Hannah soon discovered only God could help her. The doctors offered nothing. Her friends had given up. Even her own husband, who was normally supportive, finally came to the place where he said, "Am I not better to you than ten sons?" (1 Samuel 1:8). Hannah found there was only One who could do anything about her problem.

Although God seemed to refuse to bless, to say "No" to her requests, Hannah kept coming back year after year. Same prayer. Same requests. Same hope. Same answer—but she didn't give up.

Many of us fall prey to a Satanic ploy that says, Well, I prayed about it. God didn't answer. So I guess it's not His will. And we give up. But is that what God intends?

The lack of a speedy answer to prayer is no reason for laziness in prayer. Many times we see people in Scripture pleading with God, believing they could influence His decisions. It wasn't that they thought they could change His eternal will. They didn't know His will! No one knows God's eternal will until it's history. There is no reason ever to think, *Whatever He wants will be. So why pray?* Instead we need to say, "This is what I want, Lord. You said ask—so I'm asking."

Prayer is like going to court. Imagine a lawyer appearing before the judge for an innocent man in danger of the electric chair. Suppose he said, "Well, I'd really like you to acquit this man, Judge. I don't think he's guilty. I suppose I could tell you my reasons. But I know you already know them, so why go into it? Anyway, it's up to you. Whatever decision you make, we'll accept."

I'd fire that lawyer. I want a fellow who gets the facts, shows why the verdict should be in the prisoner's favor, and pleads with all his soul for mercy and justice. When we pray we ought to be as persuasive and fervent as if we were a mother trying to get some food for her starving children. Hannah came before God with words that seared her heart. She sought to sear His. She had learned to seek God with passion. Do you seek God with fire, fervor, vigor? Or do you meander in, plop down, murmur out a request, and go your own way for the next six months?

As a sophomore in college in 1970 I wanted to buy a car. My father and I talked about it at length.

Dad said, "So what kind of car do you want?"

I didn't hesitate, "An MGB."

He frowned. "You won't get good mileage, you know. And its only a twoseater—only one passenger on trips to and from school. Plus MG's are notorious for always being in the garage."

71

I didn't like it but it made sense. I began searching around. In the process I found an MGB. I told Dad, "It's great. I got the guy down to $1350."

"You'd need a loan."

"Right."

"Where will you get one?"

I gave him a long, mournful look, then gave up.

After that we cruised around the used car lots looking for my dream machine. One lot featured a 1959 Dodge. "A good family car," the salesman told us. Dad liked it. "It'll get good mileage. Has lots of room."

But I nixed it. "It looks like the kind of car a nerd drives." Strangely, Dad agreed. "I guess you want something more sporty." Now I knew he was with me.

Then one day someone called up and told Dad about a lady who was selling a 1965 white Ford Mustang. "Four on the floor, 289 four-barrel, less than 40,000 miles. Cream-puff condition. It's for you." He raced me over. We checked it out, drove it around. Oh, man, I had to have it. We bought it and I screeched off into the sunset.

I often think of seeking God's blessing as like that time with my Dad. It's a working together. There's give and take. There's discussion, examination, hope, despair, a crisis, a climax. Prayer is an earnest discussion between two persons who love one another. You work out a solution to a problem that both believe is the wisest course. Hannah may never have learned to pray with power if she had not gone through years of disappointment.

ALLOWS US TO RECEIVE GOD'S BEST

Lacking God's blessing for a time may lead to far greater blessing up ahead. Have you ever thought about all the stupid things we do to avoid pain, hardship, effort, and expense? We have a problem and want a pill. We skip a meal and feel as if we've set McDonald's on fire. We stick with the junior boys' Sunday school class for six months and think we're ready to be included in Hebrews 11.

But God loved Hannah so much He wouldn't give her second best. He could have landed six kids in her lap by the age of sixteen. But He made her wait for a reason. He wanted her to bear a Samuel, not just some nameless kid like Peninnah's boys. A Samuel, the prophet of God. Sometimes God's best blessing is the one preceded by the greatest pain. God loves us too much to let us get the goods too easily.

My friend Bill Scott told me about a birthday he had as a child. For years he had begged his parents for a horse. But as time wore on, he gave up on it. Shortly before his twelfth birthday, his Dad asked him what he wanted. "Blue jeans," he said.

When he pranced downstairs on birthday morning, he was ready to tug on those blue jeans. But his father simply asked him to go out to the barn. Bill asked where his present was. "You'll get it," Dad said. "But go out to the barn first. Make sure there's plenty of hay."

Bill was upset. He wanted those blue jeans. He threw such a corker that Dad finally said to Mom, "We'd better get this guy some blue jeans." She rushed him out and bought a pair.

Now dressed in his Levi finery, he was ready for the barn. He ambled out and discovered a horse in the stall by the hay, saddled and ready to go. He rushed back to the house and shouted, "There's a horse out there." "Right," said Dad. "It's yours, Bill. For your birthday." Bill was astonished. He'd set his sights on blue jeans—and his father wanted to give him a horse.

You have to think about that. We fight God all the time about such things. We want what we want when we want it! And God doesn't want to give us what we want. He wants to give us the things we can only dream about.

What blessing are you seeking now? How long have you waited? Two years? Five? Ten? Maybe you need to ask, "What is God trying to give me that I haven't even thought about?"

SEEKING GOD'S BLESSING

I can picture you as you read right now. You're saying, "Great. Just great. I understand all the reasons why I don't have God's blessing. What do I do while I'm waiting on God? How do I stand firm?"

For one, *make sure it's a legitimate blessing.* Hannah didn't want a VCR or a pink Cadillac or a third house on a river. She wanted a child. This was something God clearly said was His will for married women. He told Adam to "be fruitful and multiply" (Genesis 1:28). One might plead this verse alone in asking for children.

Yet many saints seek illegitimate blessings. David looked on Bathsheba and wanted her. Ahab gazed at Naboth's vineyard and had to have it. James and John wanted seats at the right and left hand of Jesus. But God does not say, "Delight in Me and I will give you the passing (or "sinful," "greedy," "materialistic," "lustful") whims of your heart." He says, "Delight yourself in the Lord; and He will give you the desires of your heart" (Psalms 37:4). First, there must be delight. Then the granting of one's desires.

Ask yourself, "Why do I want this blessing from God?" So you can "spend it on your pleasures" (James 4:30)? Or is it to advance your relationship with God, to spread His kingdom, to meet a need He Himself has created in you (such as becoming a mother, finding a mate, getting food, paying for a son's education)?

Another step is to *work to meet your need in a legitimate way.* Hannah prayed. She sought the Lord. Her husband offered special sacrifices. Many people have honest needs, but they try to meet them by their own means. Abraham listened to Sarah, took Hagar to bear a son, and in the process created the rivalry we know today between the Jews and Arabs. Similarly in Acts 5 Ananias and Sapphira sought respect and acceptance from their peers, but they tried to get it by deceiving Peter and the elders. They sought good blessings by improper means. Never in God's kingdom does the end justify the means.

A married woman who seeks "fulfillment" might go the career, divorce, or promiscuous route, all to an unhappy end. A businessman might use deception, finagling, or threats to get his way. But any method that is clearly dishonest or unscriptural is the way to death. Again, ask yourself, "Am I seeking this blessing by the wrong means?"

A third step is to *seek God's blessing in His time.* Hannah was willing to submit to God's plan. Yet some Christians who seek a blessing and can't get it refuse to recognize Christ's lordship. They can't wait till later. It's got to be now. But Peter reminds us, "After you have suffered for a little while, the God of all grace, who called you to His eternal glory in Christ, will Himself perfect, confirm, strengthen, and establish you." (1 Peter 5:10). Again, ask, "Am I willing to wait on God's timing?"

A fourth step is *the possibility of making a vow.* Hannah made a deal with God. "Give me a child," she said, "and I'll give him back to you as a Nazirite." Some would consider this blasphemous. "God makes no deals!" they shout. "You can't bargain with God."

True or not, Hannah offered God a plum if He would give her a son. In some ways, it doesn't look like such a tough deal. But have you ever tried to make a deal with God?

When we talk about making a vow to God we usually think of the businessman who gets trampled in a financial stockquake and prays, "God, if you get me out of this, I'll go to church for the next ten Sundays!" Or the foxholed soldier who squeals as the shells whine over him, "Just let me live, God, and I'll be a priest (or minister, missionary, choir boy)."

But when you look at the vow Hannah made, there are some important differences from the typical "deal." For one, she arrived at this deal only after years of seeking. It was her last hope, so to speak. Perhaps she had considered other vows, but this was her highest offer. It was no shout in the dark or prayer on a whim. This was the final plea of a broken saint.

For another, this vow came out of a long and close communion with God. From Hannah's prayer in 1 Samuel 2:1-10 we see this was no ordinary woman. She was a woman after God's own heart. She knew Him intimately. She "delighted in the Lord." So He gave her the desires of her heart.

Last, this vow cost her everything. She knew exactly what it meant. It was not something she could shrug off five years later saying, "It was just foolishness. I'm sure God understands if I don't present Samuel at the temple." No, she was making God an offer that wrenched her heart.

If you choose to make a vow, consider Hannah a prototype. God does not bargain with scamps, cheats, or liars.

GOD'S BEST ALWAYS COMES

Ultimately, the blessing came. That is, the son blessing. In fact, Hannah had four sons and two daughters in later years. But the first was a Samuel.

Hannah's lack of a blessing become one of God's greatest blessings. God withheld lesser blessings to give her the greatest of all: not just a son, but holiness, intimate knowledge of God, a sweet and gentle spirit.

While we can't be sure that God's blessing will come in a form we expect, we can be sure He'll give us His best. We may want a ministry in New York, but He may have something in mind in Australia that is far greater. We may desire a husband or wife, but He might give us a special ability to minister to singles or the aged. We might want to lead a Sunday School class that grows from ten to one hundred in a year, but He may plan to build patience and perseverance into our lives for eternity by having us work with a class of three that never grows.

It's a little like the boy who walked into the candy store and the owner decided to give him a handful of candy for free. When the man told him to hold out his hand, the boy put both behind his back. "Please put the candy in your hand, sir," he said, "and then put it in the bag." The candy man was a little perlexed, but kindly poured out a handful of candy into his hand and dumped it all in the bag. He asked, "Why did you ask me to take out the candy?"

"Because you have a bigger hand!"

Whose blessing would you rather have—the one you can dream up, or the one the omniscient, almighty, wise, loving, and infinitely gracious Lord of all can dream up? Then put your hands behind your back and ask Him to give you a blessing the size of His own hands. That is what He brought Hannah to. Don't you want Him to bring you there also?

I'm amazed at all the trouble
God went to with this rebel.
The storm was difficult enough.
Keeping it focused on this one ship.
Whipping it higher and higher.
People can't even forecast weather,
let alone make it.

Then having the lots come out
right on Jonah. Nothing left to chance
on that one. What if there had been
a tiny mistake? The wrong man
might have ended up in the fish.
Consider explaining that.

The fish, too. God must have
made him up special. The perfect
return trolley for God's man.

Then the gourd growing in one day.
Lots of supernatural fertilizer I suppose.
And hustling the worm over
to kill the gourd.
All just to illustrate a truth.
I never saw a Sunday school teacher
go to such lengths for a mere object lesson.

It's amazing the trouble God went to
to get this bigot headed straight.
Does He care that much?

5

Jonah:

"I'D RATHER DISOBEY"

I lay in bed thinking about the disagreement my wife and I had just had. Several Scriptures flitted through my mind. "Be angry and yet do not sin; do not let the sun go down on your anger."

Enough of that one.

Then, "Husbands, love your wives, just as Christ also loved the church and gave Himself up for her."

"No," I told myself. "I'm not giving in."

In rapid succession other verses plinked into my mind. "Confess your sins to one another." "Honor one another." "Husbands, love your wives, and do not be embittered against them."

I lay there trembling and angry. "She's just being stubborn. Why should I cater to her. I'm going to wait—even if it takes three hours."

"Blessed are the peacemakers."

"Why do I have to be first?"

Again the relentless inner voice spoke. "However you want others to treat you, so treat them."

I banged my fist on the dresser. "I'd rather be mad." My conscience and I battled back and forth for a good ten minutes. Finally I hauled myself out of the bedroom and ambled into the living room. "I'm sorry, Honey. Will you forgive me?" She nodded. Soon we were hugging one another. As I walked back to the bedroom, something within me whispered, "Wasn't that a lot easier than not speaking for three hours?"

I smiled and sagged into bed, glad everything was settled.

THE RIGHT THING IS OFTEN THE HARD THING

Isn't it incredible how hard obedience is—even when you know what's right? On some issues I've argued with the Bible, my conscience, concerned people, and my own family for days—months—over whether some basic teaching of Scripture should be applied in my situation.

There have even been times when I *knew* what was right. Scripture clearly commanded it. Try as I might, there was no offbeat interpretation I could cite as evidence that my disobedience was acceptable. All the excuses I came up with did nothing to ease my prickly conscience. Yet I continued to disobey.

DIFFERENT KINDS OF DISOBEDIENCE

There are several different ways in which we can be disobedient. Disobedience is not always conscious defiance. Sometimes we slip into it without thinking. That's what I'd call *unwitting disobedience*. We're simply not aware something is wrong. We commit a sin without realizing it's even a sin.

A second kind is *unplanned disobedience*. This is the thing we do wrong without premeditation. We fall into it much as Peter fell into denying Jesus three times.

A third kind is what I'd call *unwanted disobedience*. This is the kind we don't desire or plan, but because of some wrong habit pattern we give in to it repeatedly.

A fourth kind is *misguided disobedience*. Here we find out what Scripture says on an issue, but we decide to go another route. Sometimes we honestly misinterpret Scripture and find ourselves in trouble because of that misunderstanding.

But then there's *willful disobedience*. Some situation arises. Instantly we know what Scripture says about it. We stop, momentarily wavering between going God's way and our way. Then we choose—and go the wrong way. We know it's wrong. But somehow we don't care. We're going to do what we want regardless of what God says.

There are Christians who battle God for years about such things—ministering to the poor, giving a generous share of their income, telling God yes *no matter what*, making restitution or an apology for a wrong. We know that refusing to do such things is wrong, but still we disobey. What does God say about such people? Can we ever be set free from such insubordination?

One of the grimmest examples of such disobedience is Jonah. He was a prophet living around 750 B.C. in the northern kingdom of Israel. God called him to go to Nineveh, the capital of Assyria, one of the most vicious empires ever to reign in the East. God wanted him to preach a message of doom. "In forty days I will destroy this city."

Jonah heard the Lord's message, jumped up, and ran in the opposite direction. He boarded a ship for Tarshish, a region on the coast of Spain. If you can imagine God calling a fellow in Pittsburgh to go to New York City and preach the gospel, and that fellow immediately catches a plane for Hawaii, you get a clear picture of what Jonah did.

WHY PEOPLE WILLFULLY DISOBEY GOD

Jonah's disobedience provides insight into why we willfully disobey God. Jonah knew how powerful God was. He knew God could **stop him. He knew the Scriptures, Israel's** history, the record of God's way of dealing with disobedient saints. Yet he ran from God with all the strength in his being. Why?

Like most of us, Jonah was susceptible to spiritual lunacy—doing something we know is futile, but we're so upset we'll try it anyway. Jonah ran because Nineveh was a merciless enemy of Israel. Not that Israel was any big problem for Nineveh. As far as they were concerned, Israel was a little podunk heap by the Mediterranean with little value except as a source of slaves and trinkets. But being a prophet, Jonah might also have known that Assyria would soon overrun Israel in 722 B.C. and take the whole nation into a slavery from which they would never return. Jonah simply didn't want to preach to an enemy.

But there's more to it than that. He wasn't afraid of being hurt. Otherwise, he never would have told the sailors to throw him out of the ship. Nor did the length of the journey trouble him. He was fleeing three times as far as God asked him to go. Jonah gives us the deeper reason for his insubordination in chapter four, verse two. He says he knew God was gracious, compassionate, loving, and one who forgives, and he didn't want to preach to Nineveh for fear they might repent and be saved!

Astonishing, isn't it? Here's a man whose sole purpose in being alive is to tell people about God so they can repent and have eternal life, and he's not interested in doing it. That's a tremendous insight into the reason many Christians disobey God: *They simply don't care what God says or wants; all they care about is their own selfish desires.*

That's a grim thought. We like to think of ourselves as mostly loving and kind, doing right for the right reasons. We picture ourselves as "good" people, decent, kind, willing to do as God says.

But inside of us lurks a deceitful spirit that would care for no one but ourselves except for the grace of God. Consider those times in your past when you disobeyed God. Wasn't the primary reason plain selfishness? You didn't like what God said, so you decided to do as you pleased.

HOW GOD WARNS A SINNING CHRISTIAN

We have all run up against the wall of self-will. Does God just let us walk away in the opposite direction or does

He do things to try to spin us around and send us off in the right direction? Jonah's story, in revealing just what kind of God we have, offers stout hope—and a warning—to those of us who wrestle with an ungodly nature.

Clearly, God was real and near to the prophet. Jonah 1:3 says that Jonah fled from "the presence of the Lord." Jonah ran to get away. Even though Jonah was a prophet, and God probably manifested himself to prophets in ways we can never understand, each of us has that same sense of God's presence. God speaks to us through our consience. Even though the conscience of a lost person is defiled and can be perverted, and even though a Christian can "harden" his conscience (much as a wound builds up a callous), the Lord still speaks through the "still, small voice." During Jonah's getaway, the Spirit of God must have spoken to Jonah's heart repeatedly. "Is this right?" "Should you be doing this?" Jonah shoved those thoughts away, but God often halts sinners at this point. A simple reminder through conscience stops them in their headlong sprint into sin. It's also interesting to note the difficulty Jonah had in finding a ship to Tarshish. That took time, money, energy. And it presented more opportunities for the Spirit to warn Jonah, to ask questions, to plead with him, "Stop! Don't you know you're hurting yourself? This is starting to cost." Every time Jonah dipped into his purse or stopped for a breath, the Spirit was at his shoulder, speaking, persuading, wooing. Still, Jonah found a ship and paid the money. At that point, one of the diabolical deceits struck him. I wonder if Jonah didn't think, "See, you did find a ship. God must have changed his mind about sending you to Nineveh." Or, "You need to think about this. Heading off to Tarshish is just the thing for you—you can do a little meditating before you go to Nineveh!" Ever notice how we twist things around to convince ourselves that disobeying is the right thing to do?

So Jonah scurried down into the ship's hold and fell asleep. After that, God stirred up the sea with a little hurricane. Obviously He was taking firmer steps to deal with the prophet's sin. Christians who continue in sin will always find that God heightens the ferocity of His discipline. He loves us that much.

At that point also, Jonah's disobedience had involved others. Before, it was just him and God. Now it was the whole ship and its crew. Again we see an important principle: *Sin always has side effects.* Others get hurt just by being in the vicinity of a disobedient Christian. There's a price to disobedience. In this case all the ship's goods were thrown overboard—a total loss.

Clearly God was trying to get a message to Jonah. "Repent! Stop!" While your circumstances aren't always an indicator of sin, if you're sinning, your circumstances will get rough. It's always wise to ask yourself when things keep going wrong, "Am I disobeying God in some area? Could he be disciplining me?" "Is it my problem?"

However, the storm God hurled onto the sea had no effect on Jonah. He was snoring away in the hold, drained from his run from God. The deeper a sinner gets in his sin, the more oblivious he is to what's going on around him. Sin hardens hearts. Indifference, anger, restlessness, discontentment are often signs of God's displeasure. I wonder if even Jonah's dreams didn't resound with agitation and worry. Often when I have sinned, my sleep is not a deep, refreshing sleep, but restless and throbbing.

As the storm intensified, the captain awoke Jonah and said, "How can you be sleeping at a time like this? Get up, call on your god. Perhaps your god will be concerned about us so that we will not perish" (Jonah 1:6). The captain didn't know Jonah was the cause of all the trouble. He only knew that no one sleeps when the ship is sinking. God again seems to be telling Jonah to examine himself, to ask, "Hasn't this little charade gone far enough?"

Jonah's only reaction was to saunter upstairs and blithely gaze around at the carnage. He knew why it was all happening. But he didn't care. Though God spoke to his heart, he drowned it out with a rationalization. "Maybe the sailors have also offended God. Anyway they're sailors. They should know how to deal with a little storm." What callousness! Yet that's what happens when we disobey. We become so self-centered it doesn't matter who's hurt in the process.

But the sailors were desperate, and decided to cast lots to find out who was the cause of all the desolation. This was a common way of deciding an issue in those days and might have been done by throwing dice or passing out stones. Whoever received the odd one was the culprit. The moment the lot fell on Jonah, everyone began questioning him about his homeland, work, and why God would do this. When Jonah told them that he was a Hebrew and that he was fleeing from God, the sailors became terrified. The God of the Hebrews was known worldwide for His power. They asked him, "How could you do this?" Instantly Jonah was exposed and confronted in public for his sin. When lesser measures don't work, God takes a severer course. A sinning Christian must be halted.

Jonah made no answer.

And what answer could he give? What defense can anyone give for rank insubordination? So the sailors asked, "What should we do now?" Jonah answered, "Throw me overboard."

It's a startling answer. He could have repented at this point and simply said, "Let me off at the nearest port. I'll get going to Ninevah." Undoubtedly the storm would have stopped. But this man had concrete around his heart. It's astonishing to see all the measures God used to warn Jonah—and yet they only seemed to push him further into disobedience.

I've seen such a reaction in my own life. As a teenager, one of my chores was cutting the lawn. I'd do anything to avoid it. I remember on one occasion, to try to escape my father's command to "get out there and cut it," I purposely twisted some screws on the lawnmower carburetor to put it out of commission. After a few pulls on the starter, I ambled in and told Dad, "There's something wrong with it. It won't start." He walked out and instructed me to begin pulling the starter cord. For the next half hour, I pulled the cord and he fiddled with the carburetor. Finally it started. I was exhausted. But Dad patted me on the behind. "It's okay. Now let's get cutting that lawn!"

It's amazing to me that the consciences of the sailors were more tender than Jonah's. When the storm did not stop, they called on God, asked Him not to let them perish on account of Jonah's sin, and threw Jonah overboard. The sea stopped instantly—I mean it was like the director said "Cut" and it was cut in midwave! What a testimony on God's behalf. Those sailors probably never forgot it. Even in the midst of Jonah's disobedience, God was able to display His power.

The narrative goes on to say that Jonah disappeared beneath the waves. As Jonah plunged downward into the ocean he came to his senses. Faced with death, Jonah saw himself, his sin, and God's displeasure. He cried out to God to save him. God did save him, by sending a fish to swallow him and actually rescue him from drowning. Jonah recognized he was far from God and that God was disciplining him. He was sorry he had run from God—but he wasn't sorry he hated Ninevah.

God heard Jonah's cry and saved him. Isn't that amazing? One of Christianity's marvels is that hope and rescue are always available to those who take steps to move toward God.

But repentance doesn't ensure freedom from the immediate consequences of sin. Jonah spent three days gagging on bile. His skin may have been permanently altered by the experience. He lost much time and money through his rebellion. In addition, Jonah wasn't even freed from the responsibility to obey the original call—God said, "Okay, Jonah, you've detoured about a bit, but my will hasn't changed. You're going to Nineveh."

Even more incredibly, the people to whom Jonah was going worshiped a god who appeared as a fish. What did they think when they heard how this prophet of the God of heaven emerged from a fish? That might be a key to understanding why such an amazing revival took place. Perhaps the people said that the God of Jonah was greater than the god of Nineveh. In this I see great hope. God not only saved Jonah from death and gave him his job back, but He even turned Jonah's sin to good! We see once again the truth of Romans 8:28, that God "causes all thing to work together for good"—even iniquity.

HOW GOD DEALS WITH A SINNING CHRISTIAN

God may have stopped Jonah from running away, but He still had a severe problem: Jonah's sinful heart. Jonah's real problem was bigotry. It wasn't just that he didn't want to do what God said. He hated those people—lost people, men and women "without hope and without God in this world" (Ephesians 2:12). How did God change Jonah's attitude?

STEP ONE: GOD GETS US TO OBEY OUTWARDLY

The first step for Jonah was actually going to Nineveh. Real change always begins with behavioral change. It's like what my parents used to say when I'd complain about some task I had to do. "But I don't feel like it right now." My mother would reply, "You don't have to feel like it. Just do it."

Good advice. We make a mistake when we think God expects us only to obey if we have the "right attitude." The Lord does care about motives, how we feel, what we're thinking as we do the work He's given us.

But there's a basic difference between our old nature—the way we were before we were born again—and our new nature. The old nature was guided by a corrupt mind. That mind generated feelings—desires, lusts, fears, resentments, a general attitude. In turn the mind and feelings directed the will. We did what we "felt like doing." We did "our own thing." The new nature is different. Our minds are renewed by constant exposure to God's word. We begin to think His thoughts. But here's the subtle difference. Thinking His thoughts does not immediately affect our attitude. They're still tied to the old habits and reactions of the old nature. Thus, in one breath we can think God's will is good and not want to do it emotionally. This is the whole struggle Paul refers to in Romans 7.

But that's where will comes in. We *choose* to do what's right because our mind has been renewed. Eventually, our attitude catches up. Soon, we not only choose to do God's will; we want to do it with all our being. It looks like this on paper:

> Old Nature: *Corrupt mind* produces *wrong attitudes* and leads to *sinful actions.*
> New Nature: *Renewed mind* causes us to *change our behavior* which in turn produces *good and right attitudes.*

Attitudes change as we obey despite our lack of good motives.

STEP TWO: GOD EXPOSES US TO THE OBJECTS OF OUR SIN

But while God managed to get him giving the message, Jonah still harbored his hatred. He went through the city and systematically preached the message God gave him, but it's a brief message. "Yet forty days and Nineveh will be overthrown." Why so short? I see one basic reason. Jonah was going to do what God said—and that was all. He'd obey the letter of the Law, but not the spirit of it.

Imagine what may have happened as Jonah plodded through the city shouting out his message. He saw the city. He looked into the faces of the people. He noted the bentbacked woman trudging along under her load of fruit. He saw the child with dirt on his face playing with the cobblestones. He noticed the shopkeepers bargaining, laughing, hoping. He looked into the eyes of a soldier at home on leave as he carried around his new boy to meet the neighbors.

God forced Jonah to see what he had done. God said, "Okay, Jonah, if you're going to hate these people, I'm going to make you look into their faces." What Jonah began to discover was that these people were a lot like his people in Israel, only they were lost. Perhaps it occurred to him how needy they looked and what despair they lived under. Perhaps he sensed their pain, their worry, their fear. God was trying to get Jonah to "feel something" about the people God wanted him to preach to.

I find that when I disobey, God often makes me face the consequences of my disobedience and how others see it. Several years ago I attended a crabfeast with my parent's church. A woman sat down next to me who engaged me in conversation about faith and religion. It was obvious that she didn't understand what it meant to be born again. She even remarked that she couldn't stand people who were always talking about such things. I felt a bit irritated with her cynical remarks, so I began witnessing to her rather mechanically.

In the course of our conversation, she related to me a tale of three divorces and even of one husband who was supposedly a Christian, but turned out to be a homosexual.

In the meantime, I persisted in outlining the gospel without listening very carefully to her words. I blithely painted a "pie in the sky" gospel, telling her things would work out if she turned to Jesus.

Suddenly, she became angry, saying, "You people always talk so much about everything working out. But it's totally unreal to me. I've told you what I've been through in my life, but you just keep saying the same old thing. Do you Christians ever feel anything?"

She peered at me and I found myself praying, "Lord, let me feel something for this person."

She said, "Let me tell you something, do you have any idea what it's like to be rejected by three different husbands? My last husband was a homosexual. Do you know what it's like to be a woman and to be left by your own husband because he prefers his homosexual lover to you? Do you know what it's like to live with those feelings, to hurt like that, to look at yourself in the mirror and know the man you loved rejected you for another man? Does Jesus have anything to say about that?"

Suddenly, something inside me began to feel the hurt this lady had suffered. I knew I didn't fully understand. But I hurt just to see her in such pain. I said, "Can I pray just a moment?" I didn't even say, "For you."

She said, "Go ahead, but I don't think it'll do much good."

I began praying and suddenly I began weeping, pleading with God to show her his comfort and let her know of his love. In that moment her pain became my pain. Suddenly, I saw her as God saw her, a desperately hurting, broken person in need of the love and acceptance only divinity can offer.

When I finished, she searched my eyes with astonishment, then said, "Now I know you're for real. Tell me the gospel again."

STEP THREE: GOD SEEKS TO GET OUR ATTITUDE OUT IN THE OPEN

But Jonah's heart remained hard. If he recognized the need of the people, he slung it away. He became even more hardened in his hate. At the same time, the people repented. The greatest revival in history occured. God relented and decided not to destroy the city. And then Jonah became furious.

Again, it's astonishing. Isn't this the thing a preacher dreams about? Jonah never saw a response like this in synagogue. This was the very thing he thought would happen and the thing he wanted to prevent. He went out on the bluff overlooking the city and began complaining to God. He wanted to see those people burn.

Well, at least he was honest. He told God exactly how he felt: "I'd rather die than be a witness to this."

You have to admire that honesty. Are you that honest with the Lord? It's a key to dealing with disobedience. God wants us to share everything with Him—even our negative feelings about Him and His will.

Then the Lord asked Jonah a simple question, "Do you have good reason to be angry?" In other words, "Okay, Jonah. I understand your feelings. I'm willing to listen to whatever reasons you have for them. Let's discuss it."

Again, God was trying to transform Jonah. So he took this third step. He had to get Jonah's attitude out in the open. Notice that this is the first time Jonah has admitted his real feelings. Though God knows all about them, He has to lead us to the place where we're willing to admit them!

This is critical to changing wrong attitudes. Through getting us to air our feelings and set all the internal grit on the table, we are enabled to begin dealing with those feelings. God wants us to deal with the gunk, not shovel it into a closet.

This is why confession of sin is so crucial to transformation of life. We tend to think that the way God transforms sinners is through some "holy zap." But the Lord never forces anything upon us. He wants us free. He wants us to be like Jesus—complete individuals who obey from the heart. It's through confession of sin that we're set free.

No longer are we trying to hide it. No longer are we, like Adam and Eve, covering it up with fig leaves. Rather, we're like the little child who bruises himself and comes running to Mommy, saying, "Help. Look what happened!" When we get the problem out into the light, it can be properly treated and healed. God always honors genuine repentance and petitions for help.

STEP FOUR: GOD BEGINS TO REVEAL HIMSELF

Just the same, though Jonah had confessed his feelings, he was still angry. He knew his attitude was wrong. He couldn't argue with God. But he decided he would sulk. He went out to the edge of the city, made a sunbreak for himself, sat under it, and watched. He was waiting for God to destroy the city.

In actuality, Jonah was trying to manipulate God. "If you won't do it my way, Lord, then I'm not going to like you! In fact, I won't even speak to you. I'll sit here till you do act the way I want."

But God, as always, was patient with Jonah as He is with us. What He wanted to do was renew Jonah's mind—make Jonah see things as God saw them. He decided to give Jonah an object lesson. First, He miraculously grew this gigantic gourd. This was a leafy plant, the kind which always seems cool when you sit by it. It was God's way of air conditioning Jonah.

Instantly, Jonah was pleased. First, because he was no longer sweating it out up there. Second, because he thought God had finally come over to his side. For a whole day, Jonah lolled in the cool and told himself how good God was. He convinced himself that it wouldn't be long until God destroyed the city.

But God's lesson wasn't over. He sent a worm which killed the plant in only hours. Then he whipped up a "scorching east wind" and cranked up the sun till Jonah was pouring sweat like a horse in gallop. Jonah again begged God to kill him, this time because the plant died.

Then God asked Jonah, "Do you have good reason to be angry about the plant?"

Jonah said, "I certainly do, even angry enough to die." Now God came to the real issue. He said, "You had compassion on that plant which you didn't work for, didn't nurture or cultivate, and which came up in one day and died in one day. Now shouldn't I have compassion on Nineveh, which has over 120,000 babies as well as many innocent animals and beasts?"

What was God doing? Trying to renew Jonah's mind by revealing His heart to Jonah. Through giving Jonah the gourd, He enabled Jonah to identify with His outlook on Ninevah. He didn't blast Jonah's mind with laser therapy. He didn't twist the prophet to force him into a new mold.

Too often I think of the process of discipline and the renewing of the mind as a sudden, catastrophic thing. If we don't do as God says, He'll ram us through. He leads us step by step, but ultimately leaves the decision up to us.

As unbelievable as it may seem, there is no indication in Scripture that Jonah's attitude was changed by what God showed him. We don't know if he went back into the city and lived among the people—we never hear about him again. (But since Jonah is credited as the author of the book, many believe he repented.) But we do know that regardless of Jonah's attitude, God's will was accomplished. Jonah did go to Ninevah and the city did repent. I find comfort in knowing that my disobedience will not thwart God's purposes.

We know also that God was infinitely gentle with Jonah. He guided him, wooed him, put his arm over Jonah's shoulder and said, "Let's talk about it. Let's work this thing through." He gave Jonah countless opportunities to repent.

I love that about our heavenly Father. He never compromises the image of Jesus for a facelift. He wants us to think as He thinks and do as He does, but He'll never coerce us.

We've looked at several different reasons people obeyed God so far in this book. Moses obeyed because he saw God's power. Abraham obeyed because he trusted God.

But there's another reason—to obey Him because we've seen how He feels about people, because we know His heart, because we understand that grace, that kindness, that compassion, that all-encompassing love that says, "I love you and want your highest good with all my being." And because we've come to the place where we think and feel the same way. We've become like Him. For what did God want from Jonah? What does He want from us all?

Instant obedience?

A right attitude?

No, much more. He wants us to see His heart, to see how much He loves lost people, to see how much He cared about disobedient children like Jonah, to see the ache He feels when people hate and kill and lie and steal.

It's scary.
You look at Peter: brawny, tough,
tried to walk on water. As close to Jesus
as you can get.
Yet he denied Him. Three times.
And to slave girls no less.

It's scary.
It could happen to me.
I might be at work.
The boss calls me in.
He hates the Bible, Christians, God.
He says, "I hear you're a Christian,
Johnson. That true?"
I could get so frightened,
I'd say no before I even thought about it.

Or I might be out witnessing.
Some big, muscular type listens and agrees,
then says with a sneer, "But you don't think
He was God, do you? Not God?"
I could shake my head before
my mind's even thinking straight.

It's scary.
What if I did that?
What if it simply crept up on me
and pounced?
What if it happened when I wasn't prepared?

Still, I have to go back to Peter.
Jesus came to him after three denials.

6

Peter:

"I REALLY BLEW IT THIS TIME"

Roy Riegels had a chance at fame and glory on New Year's Day, 1929. The University of California was playing Georgia Tech in the Rose Bowl. Near the end of the first half, Georgia Tech fumbled. Riegels picked up the ball and ran sixty-five yards toward the goal line. The wrong goal line!

A teammate tackled him only yards away from scoring for Georgia Tech.

With backs to the wall, UC made no progress, tried to punt, and suffered a blocked kick. Georgia Tech scored a two-point safety.

Moments later, the UC players and Coach Nibbs Price filed into the locker room for the halftime talk. Riegels wrapped himself in a blanket, sagged into a corner, and wept.

The locker room was quiet that thirty minutes. When the three-minute warning came, the coach glanced at Riegels, and said to the players, "The same team that played the first half will start the second."

Everyone hustled for the door except Riegels. The coach shouted to him, "Riegels!"

No movement. The coach walked over and asked kindly, "Roy, didn't you hear me? I said, 'The same team that played the first half will start the second.'"

Riegels raised his blotched eyes and replied, "Coach, I can't do it. I've ruined you. I've ruined the University of California. I've ruined myself. I couldn't face that crowd in the stadium to save my life."

Coach Price touched Roy's shoulder. "Roy," he said, "get up and go on back; the game is only half over."

People who watched the game later remarked that no one ever played harder than Roy Riegels did that second half.

I look at a story like that and say, "What a mistake!" And then, "But what a coach!"

Have you ever failed like that?

Oh, the pain. The embarrassment. The agony of facing those we've failed. If we could just die right then we'd live happily ever after. We find ourselves praying, "Lord, never let me do that again."

Yet our lives are often filled with mistakes, miscalculations, errors of judgment that can cost us far more than a moment of humiliation, though that is bad enough. Sometimes our jobs, our homes, our very lives are the price of a bad decision.

Whenever I find myself in such circumstances, there's one person in Scripture I always turn to: Peter. You remember his blowout, don't you? Three times he denied Jesus. That wouldn't have been so bad if it had been at swordpoint or under threat of crucifixion. But this was just casual conversation with slaves and servant girls. Worse, it followed Peter's vow of absolute loyalty and courage. Mark records that "Peter kept saying insistently, 'Even if I have to die with You, I will not deny You!'" (Mark 14:31). Nothing is more difficult than facing those to whom we've just made an impassioned boast.

DIFFERENT KINDS OF FAILURE

What happened to Peter? Was this a conscious act of

rebellion on his part? Was he the unfortunate victim of circumstances?

I can't see Peter's failure as an act of willful rebellion like that of Jonah. Peter's mistake was the kind that creeps up on us subtly, then pounces and tears out our heart. We feel like a driver moving through thick fog. The accident strikes on our blind side. The next thing we know we're waking up in a hospital bed, saying "What happened?"

This doesn't excuse Peter from responsibility for his actions. He made a number of errors that led to this crash. If we can understand those errors, we can gain much insight into the reasons we fail. Then we can look at some wonderful words of hope for those who do fail.

HUMAN ERRORS THAT GO BEFORE A FALL

What led to Peter's fall? Peter was a committed, determined man capable of feats of courage beyond any of the other disciples. He possessed high spiritual insight into who Jesus was and Jesus' mission in life. But he was also brash, impulsive, given to grandiose assertions of faith, as well as asinine misstatements under pressure.

On the night of the betrayal, Peter was alone. He had also suffered a severe rebuke by Jesus when he pulled out a sword and lopped off a slave's ear. Undoubtedly that unnerved him. Furthermore, it was late, after a long day. He must have been dead tired. These factors worked together to make Peter highly susceptible to fear and errors of judgment. But, as I see it, Peter made four other critical mistakes that set him on the road to doom.

MISTAKE #1: FAILURE TO UNDERSTAND

Peter's first mistake was completely misunderstanding Jesus' purpose as the Messiah. Remember when Jesus told the disciples he had to die? Peter took Jesus aside and rebuked Him, saying, "God forbid it, Lord. This shall never happen to You" (Matthew 16:22). He was saying, "This is plain pessimism, Lord. We're going to set the world on fire.

We shouldn't think negatively." Though Jesus answered, "Get behind Me, Satan," Peter never got the message. When Jesus did die, Peter sank into despondency.

Later, when Jesus informed the disciples that they'd all desert Him, Peter was outraged. He was sure he'd fight to the death, and to prove it he whipped out the sword when the soldiers came and began flailing away. Again Jesus rebuked him.

Take a moment and analyze your own failures. Aren't they often generated by gross misconceptions about God's purposes and goals for His kingdom and your life? For instance, when I took a position as a youth pastor in a church in Indiana, I had some high hopes of what would happen. Kids would hear me teach. They'd get turned on. The group would grow. And in no time we'd have two or three hundred teenagers whipping through the city spreading the good news and turning sinners into saints.

But the Lord had other plans. Before He could ever employ me in such a way, He had to mold me, conform me more to His image. I went through some difficult times that ultimately led to my leaving that ministry. Now I see that God was shaping me in ways I have to be grateful for.

If we want to succeed with Jesus in this life, we must understand what He's doing. If we don't, we'll be working against Him. Peter hadn't grasped that, and as a result he made poor decisions about how to align himself with the plan.

MISTAKE #2: FAILURE TO HEED JESUS

Peter's failure to understand Jesus' plan led to a second error of judgment: He failed to take Jesus' words to heart.

Jesus told Peter, "Satan has demanded permission to sift you like wheat." What was Peter's response? Not self-examination. Not prayer for wisdom. Not even a cry for help—"Oh Lord, if that's the case, please help me. I know I can't stand up to him." Rather, Peter thought, "The Lord's wrong about this one. I could never deny Him."

That's the most dangerous thing of all in this world—to

know what God says and not take it seriously. Do you rationalize away commands from God, saying, "It doesn't apply to me"? Or, "This is the twentieth century. We've gotten beyond those ideas"? Anytime we learn God's word on an issue and then fail to apply it, we give Satan a foothold. He'll turn that attitude into failure for us every time.

Instead, Scripture warns us to examine our hearts. "Be all the more diligent to make certain about His calling and choosing you; for as long as you practice these things, you will never stumble" (2 Peter 1:10). Did Peter have his experiences in mind when he wrote these words years later?

MISTAKE #3: UNDERESTIMATING SATAN

When Peter neglected to take Jesus' words to heart, another mistake entered in: He underestimated Satan. Peter probably told himself, "Ha! Satan's no trouble for me. He could never get me to deny Jesus." He thought he was invincible.

This was an essential ingredient of Peter's lack of readiness. He wasn't prepared for battle because he had an unrealistic picture of his enemy.

More importantly, this unrealistic picture destroyed his ability to anticipate Satan's attack. What did Peter think would happen? Probably that a group of soldiers would come with swords and threaten him with death if he said he believed in Jesus. So Peter packed up his own sword and said, "I'll show them."

But how did Satan do it? Oh so subtly. He sent a few slaves who engaged Peter in casual conversation. Peter was already afraid, tired, and discouraged. Then Satan struck. Suddenly a slave girl in the group points to Peter and says, "He's one of Jesus' disciples." Everyone stares as Peter freezes. Prickles of heat fire up his back. His temples beat loudly; he feels dizzy. Before he's even thought through an answer, he's denying everything. "I am not. I never saw him before."

When the group saunters over and surrounds him, picking up on his Galilean accent, Peter becomes so terrified he begins cursing. As he stands there sweating, the cock crows. Instantly he turns and looks at Jesus in the inner room and he remembers Jesus's words about the denial. He runs out and weeps.

Do you realize how formidable Satan and his cohorts are? I find there are times when I feel spiritually hot. I'm at peace. Joy flows and I love everybody. Nothing gets me down. I begin to think I can handle anything. That's just when Satan loves to attack. The moment we think we've got him whipped, he pops up and starts biting our backs. God wants us to realize, "Without Me, you can do nothing" (John 15:5).

MISTAKE #4: HE BECAME PROUD

But all these mistakes led to a final error that sealed Peter's doom: He became cocky, proud. We've seen this before in Peter. Remember when Jesus asked him who he thought Jesus was and Peter said he was the Christ? Jesus commended Peter. And it all went to his head. In the next breath Jesus told the disciples he was to die, and Peter took Jesus aside and rebuked him. He had a tendency to become foolishly brash whenever he did anything important. Right before Peter's denial the Lord had told him that Satan would sift him like wheat. All he could think was that he had to show Jesus how bold he was, that he could never deny Him. He had to prove Jesus wrong!

Whenever a Christian begins to think he's temptation-proof, or has to "prove something" to others (or to the Lord), or becomes so confident he thinks he can do anything, he's in terrific danger. "Let him who thinks he stands take heed lest he fall" (1 Corinthians 10:12).

FOUR ASTONISHING FACTS OF THE
CHRISTIAN LIFE

But this is only the human perspective of Peter's failure. What about God's perspective? How did God see this situation? While Peter's human failures can lead us to despair—

which of us hasn't made the same mistakes he did?—the Scriptures offer great hope from God's vantage point.

This is where four of the most incredible facts in Peter's situation come into play. Read through Jesus' words to Peter in Luke 22:31-34:

> "Simon, Simon, behold, Satan has de-
> manded permission to sift you like wheat;
> but I have prayed for you, that your faith
> may not fail; and you, when once you
> have turned again, strengthen your
> brothers." And he said to Him, "Lord,
> with You I am ready to go both to prison
> and to death!" And He said, "I tell you,
> Peter, the cock will not crow today until
> you have denied three times that you
> know me."

FACT #1: SATAN CANNOT TOUCH US APART FROM GOD'S PERMISSION

Jesus says Satan had to get "permission" from God to attack Peter. In other words, Satan couldn't touch Peter unless God let him! Furthermore, Jesus says Satan had to *demand* permission. This isn't something God ever grants lightly. Satan can't simply bound in, make a request, and get it. I get the idea from this that he had to plead, argue, threaten, shout, scream, and whatever other verbal things a devil does to get his way.

We know this kind of situation happened before. When Satan appeared before God's throne in Job 1, he was outraged that God wouldn't even let him sneeze in Job's direction. Satan complains, "Does Job fear God for nothing? Hast Thou not made a hedge about him and his house and all that he has, on every side?" (Job 1:9-10). Satan was incensed that he couldn't penetrate this "hedge." He felt God was being unfair. When God did grant Satan permission, He set certain limits on Satan so that first he couldn't hurt Job personally, and the second time he couldn't kill him.

What marvelous words of hope! When I was first a Christian, I lived for a period in terror of Satan. Misguided Christians warned me about his power. When harsh circumstances began knocking me about, I was so afraid of him I began sleeping with a Bible under my pillow.

Yet no Christian need ever fear that Satan has power over us to cause us to fail, lose our faith, or suffer harm. Satan can't touch us unless God allows it. Jesus was saying the believer is *totally* in God's hands. We can be afflicted by anyone or anything only on God's terms, not theirs.

FACT #2: JESUS PRAYS FOR US THAT OUR FAITH
MAY NOT FAIL

Notice again what Jesus tells Peter. "I have prayed for you, that your faith may not fail." Jesus didn't say, "I have prayed that you may not fail" but "that your faith may not fail." That's a critical difference, isn't it? Jesus wasn't concerned in the least that Peter would fail Him. He desired only that Peter's faith remain intact.

You see, He knew Satan wanted to get Peter to deny his faith. Satan thought that if he could get Peter to make such a monumental mistake, he would give up the faith. He'd say, "I'm not worthy to follow Jesus. I'll go back to fishing." Or he might even follow the steps of Judas and hang himself. Regardless, Satan thought he had it all worked out: Get Peter to deny Jesus and he'll be so trampled by guilt that he'll give up being a disciple.

Just the same, Jesus also had a plan. He was praying that Peter's faith wouldn't fail. Could Jesus ever pray anything that God wouldn't grant?

FACT #3: OUR FAILURES ARE A MEANS TO
SPIRITUAL GROWTH

This passage becomes even more encouraging when we notice Jesus assuring Peter that He plans to use Peter's failure for good. He says, "And you, when once you have turned again, strengthen your brothers." After Peter fails and then repents, he'll become better able to strengthen and encourage the other disciples! That's a wonderful principle, isn't it? Nothing is wasted, not even our mistakes. Jesus will use everything for good and His glory. As we saw with Jonah, nothing we do can mess up God's plan. He's already worked it out in advance.

Just how did God use Peter's failure for good? I see two important developments in Peter's life after his mistake: God taught Peter how needy he was, and he taught him to rely on God alone.

Think about it a moment. Most of us tend to fluctuate between two extremes: haughty self-confidence and total lack of confidence, depending on our present levels of achievement and our mood. While we may not go up too high or down too low in general, few of us ever get to the point of even sailing. If we do, it's momentary.

Before this trial Peter had begun to picture himself as quite the man of God. He was part of the inner circle, one of Jesus' closest friends. He would reign in the new kingdom. He saw Jesus come into Jerusalem that Sunday with everyone shouting "Hosanna!" and suddenly Peter began to think he was really something. "Oh, yeah, I'm one of Jesus' disciples. Been with him for over three years now. We're going to start the Messianic Kingdom." Now go to Peter's feelings moments after his failure. What do you see this time? He must have been telling himself, "You crumb. God could never forgive you for this." It's the old yo-yo effect— up one moment, down the next.

But Peter needed to see that all his wisdom, works, elaborate plans, and crafty ideas were useless apart from Jesus. Once he did, the overpowering pride that caused him to speak without thinking and to act without praying would die. God allowed Peter to fail so that he could see how truly weak he was. He was humbled. When Peter saw himself as totally needy, his sense of weakness drove him to God's grace and love. This was why Paul in his affliction could say, "When I am weak, then I am strong" (2 Corinthians

12:10). Human weakness causes us to rely on divine strength, to rely on God alone.

FACT #4: OUR FAILURES ARE PART OF GOD'S PLAN

While it's encouraging to know God was in control and that Peter's failure would all turn out for good, we still can't miss one glaring fact: Satan did gain God's permission to "sift him like wheat." We're astonished. "You mean, God put Peter into Satan's hands?" Yes.

How can this be? Clearly, while the Lord protects us from Satan and limits his influence on us, there still are times when He allows Satan to attack us in a special way. Paul even told the Ephesians to "take up the full armor of God, that you may be able to resist in the evil day"(6:13). When Paul says, "the evil day," he means some special time of trial, as though Satan said to his cohorts, "Let's put aside our other duties and ask God if we can wipe out so and so today!" They tramp up to heaven and ask God permission. Most of the time He says, "Forget it!" But then there's that "evil day."

Does that mean God is evil or sanctions evil? No. He can't be tempted by evil and doesn't tempt anyone (James 1:13).

Does it mean Peter could blame Satan or even God for his error? Again, no. Peter was responsible for his failure. In fact, Jesus had done everything to prevent him from failing. Jesus had discipled him for three years. He had warned him there was great danger. He had prophesied that Peter would deny even knowing Him three times.

Then does it mean God wanted Peter to fail? Never. God can't even look on evil or approve of it (Habakkuk 1:13).

Why then does God allow this?

We must understand the nature of such a test. From Satan's point of view, the test was a temptation—an enticement to evil. But from God's point of view, it was a test—a means to prove Peter's loyalty or to probe for problems that needed to be corrected.

Think of it this way. Imagine a road test on a car built by GM. GM supplies one driver and Ford supplies another. What will happen? GM will test the car to prove how well it performs. But Ford may have a different objective: It wants to prove the car is flawed enough to be taken off the market.

Now imagine Peter (or you) as the car, with two possible drivers—Satan and God. Satan gets in and wants to show how lousy the car is. That's the goal of temptation. But God's goal is either to prove the car performs perfectly, or to check it out for flaws He wants to correct. From beginning to end He plans for the car's success.

Do you realize God is capable of handling every blowout, foulup, knockdown, and mess you'll make? In fact He *knew* before you were born that you were going to make them. But He plans to use all these failures for good in your life—if you continually turn to Him in faith. They can actually be used to make us more like Jesus.

You see, it's not the failure itself that counts. It's what we do as a result of the failure. We can repent and seek to obey Him anew in faith. Or we can follow the course of others whose faith failed (perhaps they never had real faith to begin with).

Think about the kind of failure Peter experienced. It's astonishing. I could see someone like Peter denying Jesus if he had to face burning at the stake. Or beheading. Or the rack, the lions, or anything torturous. I could even imagine Peter denying Jesus in some extreme situation when he was so depressed he doubted the existence of God. But to slave girls? If Peter had denied Jesus under extreme threats and pressure, he could always make excuses: "It was a tough situation, Lord. Anybody could have fallen like that." But Peter suffered such a humiliating blowout he would never again trust his own strength or wit. Rather, he would want to live moment by moment in the power of the Spirit.

Peter learned to rely on God. He became the evangelist who led three thousand to the Lord in one day. He led the church. He loved Jesus so much that when the time came to die for Him, Peter requested to be crucified upside down because he wasn't worthy to be crucified in the same way Jesus was.

WONDERFUL LESSONS IN FAILURE

In light of these facts, Peter's failure becomes a source of incredible encouragement to us. The key is what we learn as a result of a failure. Not just that we now know how to deal with such a problem, since wisdom always comes through hard-knock experiences. But I see three fantastic lessons that were received through Peter's defeat.

God Has a Safety Line. When I was a youth pastor, occasionally I took our teenagers rock-climbing. Have you ever done that? Absolutely terrifying.

But there was really no danger. Whenever we did a climb, we would station one very alert person at the top with a special "belaying rope" about his waist. That person was roped to a rock or tree and his belaying rope was tied to the climber. While he climbed, the person at the top kept just enough tension on the rope so that if the climber slipped, he would fall only a few feet. The climber could climb without the least fear of getting hurt.

That's what walking with the Lord by faith is all about. It's realizing we have such a loving heavenly Father that He's provided the perfect safety line. With Him at the top keeping up the tension, we can't fall to our deaths.

We Can Experience Freedom in Jesus. Notice another lesson about that safety rope. While the person on top kept the rope tense enough to prevent us from falling and getting hurt, a good safety man would also allow the climber some slack so he could climb without hindrance. While the rope kept the climber from being afraid, it also gave him the freedom to do his best.

Do you see the analogy to walking with the Lord? When we know He'll catch us if we slip, we're no longer afraid of anything. We can take intelligent risks in His name because we know He is watching out for us. When we realize He's giving us a lot of slack we're free to be creative, to be ourselves, to find our own path up the mountain. That's one reason there are so many different ways to serve, love, worship, and walk with God. He doesn't force us into one mold!

Jesus Will Get Us Where He's Going. Another thing I love about rock-climbing is that everyone wants to see you get to the top. You may fall, you may get a few cuts and nicks. You may be breathing hard. Your heart may be pounding. But there's nothing quite like coming over the edge of that cliff and seeing flat ground and that smiling safety man as he reaches out his hand, saying, "Congratulations. You made it."

Do you realize that Jesus plans to get you to His heavenly kingdom and has no intention of anything else? That's joy unlimited.

HAVE YOU FAILED?

So have you failed in some way? Bad? "Oh, it was gruesome. I blew it worse than I've ever blown it in my life."

Okay. Remember, Jesus is praying that your faith might not fail, and that when you have turned, you will strengthen others. How? By telling them that Jesus forgives, that Jesus is loyal, that Jesus never deserts us, that Jesus will stick with us forever. Look back only to repent and confess your mistakes. Then look forward. The Lord still walks before you, beckoning you and saying, "Come. Follow Me. We've still got a job to do."

That's the greatest joy of all.

Imagine that you must step uninvited
into the office of a madman
with a hatchet and a will
to use it.

Imagine that he alone
can grant your request or take your life
and has a reputation
for doing both.

Imagine his mood is bad.
He'd as soon knock off your head
as dabble with your miseries.

Imagine that you stand at his door,
listening, waiting, wondering.
You have prayed, fasted, wept.
But now it has come to this moment.

Imagine turning the knob, pushing
open the door, stepping inside.

Imagine that he looks,
fixes you with his steel eye.
His hand rests on his hatchet.
You see his fingers tap the handle.

Imagine that now you must wait
without flinching
for his word,
his choice,
his will that will decide your destiny
and that of your people.

Then cease imagining.
For even now you stand at that door
if you are one of those who seek
to live
by faith.

7

Esther:

"I COULD LOSE EVERYTHING"

Esther's heart drummed as she approached the court of her husband, Ahasuerus (Xerxes), the king of Persia. Esther loved this powerful monarch. But the slightest irritation could arouse his anger. Opposition brought his curse.

She found herself praying, questioning, and dreading all at once. "What if he's angry with me? What if he does not extend his scepter? I'll be dragged away and beheaded without mercy or defense."

Hegai, loyal from the start—when Esther was selected in the beauty contest to replace the arrogant Queen Vashti—stood at her side. "Do not risk this," he said grimly. "His mood is bad. Even this morning he flung Nehashti out of his bedroom in a fit. He is not a patient man."

Esther's lip quivered. "I know you don't understand, Hegai. This is something I must do for my people."

"But you are a queen," he said. "Your people are slaves. If they die, they die."

"I still must do what is right." She gazed away.

The pause strengthened Hegai. "Just wait another day. Surely your God Jehovah can wait another day."

Esther breathed deeply. "I vowed three days. Now I must keep my vow."

She began to push open the huge, gold-studded leather door.

Hegai touched her arm. "You're sure? You're sure your God will give you mercy in the sight of the king?"

Esther shook her head. "No. I'm not sure. Not sure at all."

He pressed more firmly. "You can't go. I won't let you go. You may die."

Esther closed her eyes. "If I die, I die."

She stepped into the throne room. And so Queen Esther set in motion great events. She took a risk that could have ended her life. But it led to glory, as we see in the book of Esther.

Have you been faced with such a risk—one that threatened your life, your family, your nation, your eternal destiny? We must be careful to set the scenario properly. We're not talking about taking a risk which is pure foolishness. Satan tempted Jesus to take that kind of risk. After planting Him on the pinnacle of Jerusalem's temple, Satan dared Him to throw Himself off and see if God sent an angel to catch Him. Satan implied this would prove His loyalty and love.

Sometimes Christians indulge such foolish whims. Some try get-rich-quick schemes, thinking God will bless them. Others neglect their families and marriages in the name of doing "a great work for God" that requires all-out time and effort. Some play with rattlesnakes and drink poison to prove God's power, and die in the process. These are risks, to be sure. But foolish risks, disobedient to the guidelines of God.

Esther's risk was what I call a "faith risk." It's attempting to solve a problem or do a work for God that is scripturally mandated and sincerely motivated. It's doing what's right in good faith, without knowing the outcome. It may involve physical or spiritual danger, and there are no guarantees from God He'll make it turn out the way we'd like.

THE NATURE OF ESTHER'S RISK

Consider Esther's situation and the risk involved. Her people, the Jews, enslaved in Babylon, were to be exterminated because the king's adviser, Haman, felt humiliated by a Jew who wouldn't bow down when he passed. Though Esther was the queen and a Hebrew, she was in great danger if her identity was revealed. To stop this mass murder, she was confronted with an even riskier circumstance. She had not seen the king for thirty days. She didn't know why—whether he was displeased about something or in a sour mood or simply preoccupied.

The only way she could gain an audience with the king was to approach him as he presided in the "inner court"—his counsel chamber. But Persian law required that anyone who came into the chamber uninvited would immediately be put to death if the king did not hold out his scepter, indicating his willingness to hear the person's request (Esther 4:11). Esther's life was in the hands of the king's mood and whim.

Moreover, the Jews' enemy was Haman, the king's most trusted counselor. It was especially risky for her since she couldn't be sure if the king would even side with her against Haman. Worst of all, no promise from God guaranteed her a favorable outcome. This was undoubtedly the hardest aspect of Esther's faith-risk: Would God make it work out? Or would she die? She didn't know. There was no way to know. The only way to find out was to take the risk of going into the inner court and making her plea.

COMPARABLE SITUATIONS

Esther underwent a trial few of us will ever face. We're not queens or kings. Nor are most of us in danger of mass murder. Yet there are comparable situations for which Esther can offer insight and direction. Consider a few.

Sharing the gospel. Witnessing to the lost involves such risks. Whether we're trekking to a distant land to live among headhunters or simply going next door to speak with the sweet lady who feeds the birds, sharing our faith is a genuine risk. We can't know the outcome. Jesus even told his disciples, "They will deliver you up to the courts, and scourge you in their synagogues" (Matthew 10:17).

Confrontation. Christians are called to confront sinners about sin. Going to a Christian brother or sister, or even speaking with an unbeliever about the need to repent, is always dangerous. Again, we can't know the response. John the Baptist was beheaded for pointing out Herod's sins. Jesus was crucified. Paul was whipped, beaten, chained, and ultimately executed because he repeatedly confronted people about sin.

Doing right. Merely obeying God's word and doing what is right is often perilous. One man I know decided not to serve alcohol in his restaurant because of his convictions. His business went bankrupt. A church in California tried to help a young man through his depression. But he committed suicide. His parents sued the church for clergy malpractice, at great legal and spiritual expense.

Speaking the truth. Standing up for truth—the inspiration of Scripture, the deity of Christ, the reality of judgment—can become a source of some of the world's harshest assaults. John Hus was burned at the stake merely because he taught God's word systematically. William Tyndale was executed for translating the Bible into English.

While such extremes aren't our daily experience, they probably happen to us occasionally. That's when we're faced with a "faith-risk." But one reason few of us are confronted with affliction or harassment in the things we're doing is because we're not doing anything risky for God!

WHY WE DON'T TAKE FAITH-RISKS

There are clear reasons why many Christians fail to take genuine risks in the name of Jesus. Satan uses three lies to prevent us from stepping out on faith.

Lie #1: *"If you go God's way, you'll lose the real blessings of life."* Satan casts up images of prosperity, success, victory, power, and honor. He tells us we'll have none of these if we go God's way. Thus, we feel if we take a risk that brings persecution or hardship, it wasn't worth it. We become bitter or give up, refusing to ever attempt anything again.

The real problem is that we're seeing things from a selfish point of view. Does life amount only to prosperity, a nice house, our names in the paper now and then, and a night out once a week? We lose the greater blessings for the false ones the devil promises.

Lie #2: *"If the door closes, God doesn't want you in it."* Many Christians operate on the principle that "wherever God wants you to go, He'll pave the way and open all the right doors." Yet, circumstances are not to be our source of guidance; God's word is. Paul encountered persecution and suffering every step of his missionary journeys. Still, he kept on going—not because every door swung wide before him, but because he had a word from God: "Go and make disciples of all nations."

Lie #3: *"If you're losing the battle, then God must not be with you".* In the fury of the fray, many Christians buckle because they're convinced that anything God is in must win. But Scripture demonstrates that when God begins a work in this world, the first things that happen are persecution, resistance, malice, ill treatment, and problems. While a door may swing open initially, there may be many punji sticks along the path.

PRINCIPLES FOR TAKING A FAITH-RISK

Once we overcome Satan's lies, we need positive guidelines for moving ahead. What principles guided Esther as she warred against the evil in her kingdom? As we unlock them, we can apply them to our own risk situations.

When Esther learned Haman's scheme for the extermination of the Jews through her uncle Mordecai, she sent her servant to tell him she could do nothing to stop it. Mordecai's reply flamed with insight: "Do not imagine that you in the king's palace can escape any more than all the Jews. For if you remain silent at this time, relief and deliverance will arise for the Jews from another place and you and your father's house will perish. And who knows whether you have not attained royalty for such a time as this?" (Esther 4:13-14). Here we find several matchless principles for biblical risk-taking.

IGNORING A RISK DOESN'T DRIVE IT AWAY

Esther might easily have reasoned, "I'm a queen. They won't touch me." But Mordecai underlines a potent thought: *Never think you can escape a risk simply by ignoring it.* We can be the world's friend today, but tomorrow it may trample us and tear us to pieces. Esther could not conceal her Jewishness forever. And Persian law would not be turned back, even for her sake. If King Ahasuerus rid himself of Vashti because she wouldn't expose herself to his drunken celebrants, neither would he flinch at signing Esther's death warrant.

When confronted with a tough situation, sometimes Christians mistakenly think, "Oh, it'll just go away." Or, "God will work it out somehow." But God may have planned to deal with the problem through us. Not only is God sovereign—in that His plan and decrees will all be worked out by His timetable and power—but we are also responsible for our actions. God has not only planned out the ends, but also the means to those ends. What if the risk we fear to take is actually the means by which God intends to solve the problem?

The truth Mordecai is pointing out is this: We can't sit back and hope someone else will take care of the problem—whether it is taking the gospel to Africa or to our neighbor, or teaching the Junior boys Sunday school class, or speaking before Congress. No, we must take action, or we will not escape when the crunch comes to us.

SUCCESS WILL COME WITH OR WITHOUT US

Some say, "But I thought God had everything under control. You mean my parents' salvation is dependent on me?" Or, "If I don't take this step of faith and move in the situation, nobody will?" Christians often place so much weight on God's power and the idea that "He will make it all turn out," that they do nothing. In this regard, Mordecai reveals a second thought: "If you remain silent, relief and deliverance will arise for the Jews from another place." What is the principle? *God will succeed with us or without us.* His plan will not be overturned by our disobedience. No one's eternal destiny is dependent on our actions. If God moves against evil, it will be stopped regardless of us.

But notice Mordecai's admonition: "But you and your father's house will perish." Yes, God's plan will succeed. But we will perish. Have you ever thought of your responsibilities before the risks of life in those terms? We tend to reason this way, "Surely God will work it out." That's true. But He wants us to be part of it.

1 Thessalonians 3:2 astounds me. Paul writes, "We sent Timothy, our brother and God's fellow worker in the gospel of Christ." Notice that Paul calls Timothy God's "fellow worker." C. S. Lewis brought this out in a poignant way in *The Lion, the Witch, and the Wardrobe.* When Aslan runs about through the evil witch's kingdom and rallies the forces of good, he says to the multitude of beasts and beings, "And now! Those who can't keep up—that is, children, dwarfs, and small animals—must ride on the backs of those who can—that is, lions, centaurs, unicorns, horses, giants, and eagles. Those who are good with their noses must come in the front with us lions to smell out where the battle is. Look lively and sort yourselves."

Everyone jumps to it, but one of the beasts, the lion, is terrifically pleased. He runs about everywhere, saying, "Did you hear what he said? Us lions. That means him and me. Us lions. That's what I like about Aslan. No side, no stand-offishness. Us lions. That meant him and me."

Think of it! God giving us equal billing with Himself. Imagine the Lord Jesus saying of you, "Yes, he and I worked side by side in the fields of harvest!" That's what Mordecai was reminding Esther of. That's how Paul saw Timothy and even himself—as God's fellow workers. That's the driving force of Christianity: Jesus enlists us as His colaborers, His joint-heirs, His brothers and sisters shoulder to shoulder in the threshing of His wheat. He wants us to share in the spoils because we've been in the battle.

GOD PUT YOU WHERE YOU ARE FOR A PURPOSE

We're apt to respond, "Does that mean I'm responsible to do everything? Should I witness to every person I meet? Am I supposed to burn myself out with chores at church? Should I feel I'm a failure unless I've gone to the corners of the globe with the gospel?"

Mordecai is helpful again. He told Esther, "And who knows whether you have not attained royalty for such a time as this?" The principle is this: *You are where you are because God put you there.* Paul told the Ephesians that God "works all things after the counsel of His will" (1:11). Later, in the same letter, he wrote, "We are His workmanship, created in Christ Jesus for good works, which God prepared beforehand, that we should walk in them" (2:10). In other words, God has a plan and has placed us in that plan at those points where we will be most effective in accomplishing His purposes. Every gift, ability, and talent, every trace of intelligence and wisdom, has been provided by Him so that we might fit perfectly into the puzzle of life.

Esther wasn't queen because she was pretty or witty. She didn't attain royalty because she used the right makeup. It wasn't charm or her freckles or her figure. Rather, it was because God had put her there. Until now, she hadn't seen clearly what God's purpose was. But now a purpose had arrived.

There are numerous examples of this throughout the Scriptures. Joseph was sold into slavery, not just because his brothers were malicious, evil, jealous, and wanted revenge, but also because God was working out the majestic plan of the ages, plotted and coordinated by the Mastermind of human history.

Pharoah's daughter raised Moses, not just because she happened to be down by the creek when his basket floated by, but because God had decreed that a leader should arise eighty years hence who would free His people.

Think of the many trivial events of your own life that have turned out to be great pivot points. God engineered those circumstances so that we might fit into His eternal purpose.

Many years ago a friend and I got high on marijuana and sat in my basement discussing religion. I had studied Christianity for some months before, but nothing in my life had changed. I casually asked my friend if he believed in Jesus Christ. He shrugged and said he didn't know. Then he asked me. It was a question I would normally answer with a joke. But something was different that night. Somehow I knew this time I couldn't be flippant, couldn't sluff it off. After a full minute's meditation, I said, "I don't know why—but I believe Jesus Christ is the Son of God." That was all. We turned to other subjects.

Over the next few days something happened inside me. I began to see as I had never seen. In forty-eight hours, questions I'd been asking about life for years suddenly had answers. I knew Jesus was the Son of God. I picked up the Bible and it made sense. I prayed, and God was real. I sensed His love and presence. And it had all pivoted on a single question in a single August evening in 1972.

What if I had pushed that question out of my mind? What if I had retorted, "Who knows about those things?" What if the question never came up? Sometimes I shudder to think of the results if I had disowned Jesus at that point. It was the critical question of my life—posed in a room reeking of pot.

If we saw every life as God does, I suspect we would see multitudes of humans put in similar circumstances and faced with similar questions and risks. Some make the wrong choice, and perish. Others—we shall know them as the "chosen of God"—we will love and praise forever.

Still we might ask, "Why am I where I am? I'm no Esther or David. What is my great task?"

On rare occasions I have played chess with men who have the ability to think five to ten moves ahead. In one situation, I was in a tight contest and my opponent moved a pawn into a seemingly useless position. I thought he'd blundered, and began to close in. But many moves later that pawn suddenly became very useful, and my opponent won the game because of its deft placement. What looked like a foolish move was actually the deciding point in the conflict.

In the same way, God is moving His pieces—you and me—throughout history. Often He places people in seemingly useless slots all their lives. They faithfully walk with Him, but nothing spectacular ever happens. Yet God is employing them in His service for reasons He alone knows. People whom the world now scorns—the little people doing little deeds in little places—will one day be heroes in heaven. Therefore, we must be ready for those opportunities when they come.

WE TAKE THE RISK BECAUSE IT'S RIGHT

Perhaps Esther wondered why she should take the risk. She could have lost everything. Mordecai's answer in 4:13-14 provides one last principle critical to the decision-making process: *We obey God and do what is right because it is right.*

Why do you do what you do? I ask myself this sometimes as I brush my teeth, or play with the baby when I have a headache, or get up at 1 A.M. and quietly listen to my wife air her feelings about something. Many times I don't "feel" like doing it. In fact, I feel like not doing it. But what is right takes precedence over what I feel at the moment.

Doing what's right because it's right can actually push us through and enable us to persevere in any circumstance.

If we know what we're doing is right (scripturally speaking), we also know God is with us. If we know He's with us, we know His victory will come, and He will bring us safely to His heavenly kingdom. This was Esther's ultimate motivation. She was afraid, she had no guarantee of the outcome, she could die; but her responsibility to do what was right remained.

Have you ever thought that this is about all God expects of us? He doesn't want us to singlehandedly turn back America from sin and evil. He doesn't say, "I want you to come up with the solution to the arms race." He doesn't shout and demand, "If you don't make a million dollars by the time you're thirty, you're no son of mine." No. All He asks is that we humbly proceed through life doing what is right at every juncture.

Isn't that incredible? I used to think I had to lead everyone on my street to Christ, become pastor of a church that grew from thirty to three thousand in six years, and have my own radio and tape ministry by the time I was thirty-five. But all Jesus says is, "Obey my word."

GOD REWARDS US ON THE BASIS OF FAITHFULNESS

But doing what's right doesn't always lead to success by the world's standards. Many Christians were consumed by lions in the Roman arenas. They did what was right, but they lost their lives. This truth may raise some hard questions.

"If I teach God's word in my Sunday school class, will the class grow?" Not necessarily. God hasn't promised that.

"If I discipline my kids and teach them the gospel, will they repent and follow Jesus?" God hasn't promised that either.

"If I stay completely honest in my business, will my business make money?" Not always.

But let's turn to one other question, a more important question, "If I obey the truth regardless of the results, will I please God?"

Absolutely. And that's all that matters. Pleasing Jesus is a priority that takes precedence over everything else. That's why the little old lady who's been faithful in teaching Sunday school will receive the same reward as the apostle Paul. *God rewards us on the basis of faithfulness, not size of accomplishment.* As a result, we need be concerned with only one thing: to please Him in all we do.

WISDOM FOR THE WAY

While seeing the truth of such principles we may still wonder, "How do I go about taking this risk scripturally? What do I do?" Esther again offers clear thoughts.

1. *Enlist the aid of God's people.* Esther called for the people to fast. Undoubtedly, this was accompanied by prayer and earnest seeking of God, though this is not stated in the test. When we face difficult situations requiring high risks, we should never act alone, though we may finally face the beast alone. We are part of a body.

2. *Don't worry about the consequences if you're doing what's right.* Esther said, "If I perish, I perish." There were no guarantees. She couldn't force or predict the outcome. She was concerned with only one thing: doing God's will.

3. *Be cautious. Proceed slowly.* Though Esther went into the king's chamber and made her request, she balked at giving her real need at the first banquet, and merely invited him to a second one. Why? It was a subtle thing, perhaps intuition or something thoroughly incomprehensible. But obviously she wasn't comfortable blurting out her request. She was cautious. She decided to hold back a day longer. Similarly, when we take great risks, we must learn to go slowly. To plod, not to sprint. Sprinters are easily tripped. Plodders go the same distance without injury.

4. *Speak the truth plainly and openly.* When Esther finally spoke, she didn't muddy her words. She hid nothing. She made the matter plain and let the knife fall as it would. In the same way we need to beware of subterfuge, trickery, or cunning in facing perilous risks. We do not go to deceive,

but to enlighten. Don't think you have to "sneak" it over on them.

5. *Once the deed is done, let God do the rest.* Esther knew she couldn't force the king's hand. She announced the truth. Now it was up to him to do something about it. When we take a risk—witnessing, confronting another about his sin, or starting a new job—we must give God time to work. Speak your piece. Then let the Spirit move.

A PERSONAL WORD

As a Christian of thirteen years I've been faced with a few heart-rending and heart-sending risks. Some have been thrilling. Others have led to great pain. But all have resulted in personal growth.

After my call to the ministry in 1973, I decided to go to seminary. I chose Dallas Theological Seminary primarily because of my desire to learn under certain men who taught there. But when I sent for an application in May for the following fall, the dean informed me, "We presently have fifteen places left in the new class and more than one hundred qualified applicants. We suggest you apply for the winter semester, or next year."

My pastor informed me of several other seminaries I might get into, even at that late date. Yet somehow I felt it was Dallas or nothing. I believed the Lord wanted me there and would get me in—*that fall.* I applied to Dallas and nowhere else. I made no other plans for the coming year. It was quite a risk.

In July I received a letter of acceptance. I was overwhelmed and overjoyed. God had honored the risk I took with a victory. My faith had grown.

Yet not all my risks have been rewarded that way. After becoming a pastor and serving several years in a church, a situation arose requiring church discipline. For over a year I tried to settle the problem, seeking to follow scriptural principles. But when the final confrontation came over what I believed was a matter of righteousness and truth, a battle ensued. I decided it was best to resign. I had no other immediate job possibilities, a tremendous hospital debt because of the birth of my daughter, and no readily marketable skills beyond the ministry. But through it all God led me into deeper faith and great love for Him and His people.

There comes a time when we must face a difficult personal dilemma: Will I do what is right according to God's word, even though I may lose everything? Or will I go another way, hoping to keep those things precious to me?

How you decide in such circumstances will show your true heart.

How long, O God?
It was in all the papers.
In the pictures he was even
smiling. Claimed innocence.
They let him off.
Some savvy lawyer spotted
a technicality.

How long, O God?
It's in the news every night.
They're strafing whole airports now.
Bombs in lockers.
Suicide missions.
They even claim You're on their side.

Don't You even care?
It tore my heart just yesterday.
The woman is paralyzed now.
And the maniac threatens that after
his sentence is over
he'll kill her.
Will You simply stand back
and let it happen?

Can't You do something—now?

8

Habakkuk:

"EVIL'S WINNING, GOD!"

Habakkuk wandered through the streets of Jerusalem as his mind seemed to scream, *It's impossible. It cannot be. Jehovah can't condone evil!*

For six months this steady-eyed, steel-spined prophet had pleaded with God. "How long will You do nothing, O God? The poor are oppressed. Thieves are everywhere. The rich take and take and take. O God, let Your hand be swift and strong. Let them not escape. Will You do nothing?"

Day after day, night after night he had sweated, stormed, and spread his heart before God.

Then God answered.

As Habakkuk walked the worn streets, he thought about what God would do. He said He was sending the Chaldeans. They were a fierce, impetuous people, galloping through the land like whirlwinds, plucking lives like figs in season. Already half the world was theirs. Reports had come in: this town burned; that settlement carried into slavery; this city annihilated, its young men slaughtered, its virgins raped.

For two days Habakkuk had been sick. He had even prayed, "I wanted justice, Lord. But this?"

131

Only the enigmatic words, "They will be held guilty, they whose strength is their god," helped him through the night. But his heart was shrieking, "How can it be? Are you not God—the Holy One, the Almighty? Can you look on evil and be pleased? Can you approve of those who deal treacherously?"

That evening he climbed the stairway to the high wall about Jerusalem and stared east. "Oh, Lord," he prayed, "please open my mind. Give me wisdom."

Suddenly, his mind was full. God was answering. The vision came in a rush, but Habakkuk's mind seemed so taut that each word sank in like a stone into a slot. The words filled him first with dread, then with a quiet mourning: "The proud are not right before Me, but the righteous will live by faith. . . . Woe to those who steal and plunder. Woe to the one who kills to gain. Woe . . . Woe . . . Woe. . . ."

A pause, and then a final word of triumph: "The LORD is in His holy temple. Let all the earth be silent before Him."

Abruptly the vision ended.

Habakkuk walked back through the city to his room. So God would punish them—all of them. All the wicked. Not one would escape. But the righteous would live on—by faith. A strange mixture of dread and hope bounced inside his mind.

As he thought about the words, he murmured, "I must write. It must all be written down. Then I'll see."

He began with the prayer for justice. Then God's first answer: the coming of the Babylonians. Next, his questions, his doubts. Finally, God's second answer: the five woes. His hand was shaking. The words flowed quickly. When he finished, he read them over and over. He kept coming back to, "All the earth will be silent before Him."

He stood and went to the window. A cool breeze struck his face and eased his tension. He began to pray: "Even if I must die, it doesn't matter. You will be exalted, Lord, and that is all that matters."

Instantly, as though a dammed river was suddenly released within him, he felt joy and hope surge through his heart.

Suddenly, he returned to his table and read the words of the prophecy again. It seemed incomplete. "This is not a message of doom," he said. "This is the greatest hope of all. Justice and mercy at once."

"I'll write a prayer," he said, "a psalm to the glory of God."

He wrote feverishly. A surging love for God burst within him like many suns glinting on the horizon. He wanted to sing. He arose and raised his arms. "Oh, God, if I could only touch You! Your radiance is like sunlight . . . rays flash from Your hands!"

As he wept and wrote, wrote and wept, he came to a final thought: "Though the fig tree should not blossom, and there be no fruit on the vines . . . yet I will exult in the LORD, I will rejoice in the God of my salvation."

"I will," Habakkuk said slowly. "I will!" he shouted. "The Lord God is my strength," he wrote. "He has made my feet like hinds' feet, and makes me walk on my high places."

Habakkuk stood, raising his arms. "You are my strength, Lord. You alone!"

HAVE YOU EVER WANTED JUSTICE?

Have you ever been enraged when . . .

> a murderer is acquitted on a technicality?
>
> a man goes in desperation to a shark loan agency, and now lives in ruin because of the monstrous interest payments?
>
> a bigot screams epithets at a member of a minority?
>
> a businessman dumps his wife after twenty

years and three children because he
needs to "do his own thing?"

Have you ever just wished God would do something
drastic to such people?

We all have. But it's often slow in coming. Many of us
have watched oppression for years with no change. Why?
Why do evil people prosper, triumph, rule, and live it up,
while many Christians look like the front end of a head-on
collision?

This was Habakkuk's complaint. His book is small, but
it was well known in Jesus' day and before. Three times
Habakkuk is quoted in the New Testament, in Romans
1:17, Galatians 3:11, and Hebrews 10:37-38. An interesting commentary on Habakkuk was even discovered among
the Dead Sea Scrolls, and in it the authors tried to prove
that their own troubled time (about 150 B.C.) was the time
Habakkuk prophesied about.

Habakkuk's theme was the cry for justice in a time of
chaos and oppression during the reigns of Jehoahaz and
Jehoiakim, two of Judah's wickedest kings. A holy man like
Habakkuk staggered in the face of such wickedness. He
cried to God for justice. But God was silent. Things only
got worse. There was "violence," "iniquity," "wickedness,"
"destruction," "strife," "contention." Indeed, how could
God let things continue, let alone be? In the process,
Habakkuk raises issues faced by all who ask, "Why does
God let evil go on?"

The first step in working through these issues is understanding whether God can and will do anything about evil
in the present. We know that one day He will judge all. But
we wonder if He does anything about wrong and injustice
while it is happening. Do we have to wait for the end to
come before oppression is stopped? Habakkuk began his record in 1:2-3 with precisely that kind of question. He said,
"How long, O Lord, will I call for help, and Thou wilt not
hear?"

"How long?" we cry. Will communism keep whacking off a piece here and a piece there? Will God never terminate terrorism? Is there any hope our children will be free of the bigotry, crime, malice, and upheaval of our times? Time and evil often seem to trudge on while God is silent.

GOD DOES JUDGE EVIL IN OUR WORLD

The first thing Habakkuk discovered was that God does judge evil in the present. In 1:5-11, God informs Habakkuk He is doing something. It's the classic case of going from the frying pan into the fire. God would discipline Judah, the southern nation, in order to turn them from their iniquity.

How? By sending the Chaldeans (Babylonians). They were fierce and impetuous warriors who dispatched their foes without forethought or afterthought. They rushed upon their victims like a horde of locusts and lopped heads like wheat before a combine. God planned to send these marauders like a huge "Stop" sign, saying, "I've had enough. I have to act. Your sin has gone too far."

Unquestionably, God does judge evil people. There is a limit to His patience. He does judge on a grand scale, as in this case. Sometimes He strikes individuals, as He did with many sinners we see in Scripture—Nabad and Abihu, King Saul, David, Ananias and Sapphira.

DO WE REALLY WANT JUSTICE?

It's interesting to note that when God does finally judge, Habakkuk is dismayed. This isn't what he meant. Sure, Habakkuk wanted justice. He longed to see Israel halted from its plunge into perdition. But this? The Chaldeans were warriors who loved violence. They mocked and laughed at anyone who opposed them, then squashed them like bugs under heel. How could God send murderous marauders to discipline these mere Hebrew extortioners? This was no mere spanking or reprimand. This was blitzkrieg raised to megathrust. This was "murder one" with

variations on rape, pillage, plunder, holocaust, and annihi-
lation. God was so severe.

It's easy to pray for justice, isn't it? But when God an-
nounces He intends to answer our prayer, we change our
minds. Habakkuk was asking earlier, "Why don't You do
something?" Now he is screaming, "How can You do that?"
God was going to make things worse!

Have you ever felt that way for your nation or your
church or even your home and friends? Suppose a Christian
friend slips away from the church, gets involved in immoral-
ity, and now lives like a pagan. We might pray, "Oh, Father,
turn him around. Please make him see the light." What if
God replied, "I'm glad you mention it, because next week
he'll be in an auto accident and will become paralyzed from
the neck down."

We're horrified. "Lord, not that! I didn't mean it."
Sure, we want justice. But not real justice. We tend to think
that when God acts against sin, He'll simply fire down a
thunderbolt into a meadow, everyone will see the light, and
suddenly people will change on the spot.

But it doesn't happen that way today and it didn't happen that way for Habakkuk. The real problem is that
Habakkuk didn't understand what it takes to turn evil
people around, to get them converted, to lead them to repentance.

Consider what God had already done to try to get Israel
into shape. He began when Moses first led them out of
Egypt by speaking kind, understanding words, giving fantastic promises, and offering them a land. But they told him
they preferred the garlic of Egypt. So He gave them the Law
to help them get along with each other. But they mocked
that Law; or worse, they pretended to obey while practicing
lawlessness in the dark. So He took firmer measures—
plagues, famines, locusts. No change. He sent prophets
with threats. But the people only slipped further into sin
and idolatry. Finally he took the whole northern nation
away into slavery, as though to say to Judah, "This could
happen to you." But still they spurned their loving Father.

Ultimately God had to take more destructive steps to stop His people. Things had gotten so bad, God decided to tear the people from the land and enslave them. In this world, God rarely deals with people on the basis of justice. We live in the midst of an incredible outpouring of grace and patience from God. In fact, we get so used to grace that when we see justice it doesn't look just! We become outraged. Many of us simply don't understand what we're praying when we plead with God for justice to be brought to our land, home, workplace, or church.

JUDGMENT IS GOD'S LAST RESORT

But now Habakkuk has a deeper problem on his hands. God would judge. He wondered, "Wasn't there some other way? Do we have to take such drastic measures?" You see, Habakkuk wanted everyone to live in peace. But he didn't understand what it took to get everyone to live in peace.

We can take heart because God not only is omniscient (knowing every detail, fact, and possibility concerning a problem), but He's also wise: He knows the best way to use that knowledge to solve a problem. Ultimately we have to ask, Which is better, for God to let people go to hell comfortably, or for Him to take whatever measures are necessary to wake them up? He loves us too much to let us destroy ourselves. If He can turn us around with moderate measures—discontentment, emptiness, fear of death—He does so. But sometimes He must take the most drastic action conceivable to win a person back.

Habakkuk was learning that God's way of solving problems isn't always our way. God not only thinks differently from us; He also acts often in ways that contradict all the reason we can muster.

Have you ever prayed for something and then gotten an answer that sent you reeling? My wife and I asked the Lord to teach us to trust Him, to make us more a man and woman of God. I figured one morning we'd just wake up, go to the mirror, and admire the shine. But what did God do? He sent us a $13,000 debt through the birth of our daughter.

Asking God to do something about evil is a dangerous prayer because the Lord will move against not only the evil within others, but all evil, including the evil within you and me.

IN GOD'S EYES, SOME EVIL IS WORSE THAN OTHERS

We also have to remember that God doesn't look at sin and evil the same way we do. We tend to think of murder, adultery, grand larceny and so on as the great evils of our age. But was Habakkuk correct in saying the Chaldeans were far worse than his own people?

To be sure, they were a nation of horse soldiers who liquidated everything in their path. But were they worse?

Consider a question: Who are worse—people who have the truth and disobey it or people who don't have the truth, but live corrupt lives anyway? Consider another question: Who made Jesus angrier—the prostitutes and tax gatherers or the Pharisees?

We must remember that God makes a special distinction among the people of Planet Earth. "To one who knows the right thing to do, and does not do it, to him it is sin" (James 4:17). God always judges more severely the people who know His truth but don't obey.

Thus, the Lord made it clear that He would take action against the evil in His nation. All of us can be sure that God will also judge the evil in our midst. His patience does not last forever. Hitler came to his conclusion, as did so many others. While they were given a small slice of time in which to repent of their evil deeds, God set the limits. When He moved against them, they were destroyed.

One theme that has come into my preaching and teaching of late is this: *Today* is the day for repentance and salvation. To people who reject Christ, live in sin, and mock the truth, I find myself saying, "You're in great danger. Time has run out! Repent today. It may be your last." After all, what was the message of John the Baptist and Jesus? "Repent, for the kingdom of heaven is at hand." They meant, "The time for procrastination and dawdling is gone. Stop! Turn around today. God may say to you, 'Tonight your soul is required of you!' "

HOW TO WORK THROUGH A DIFFICULT ISSUE

It's apparent, though, that Habakkuk still has a severe problem: Regardless of who was worse, how could God use evil—the Chaldeans—to deal with other evil—the sinning Jews?

PUT THE PROBLEM IN GOD'S HANDS

Habakkuk was stumped, but he took a wise course: *He put the problem in God's hands.* He wrote, "I will stand on my guard post and station myself on the rampart; And I will keep watch to see what He will speak to me" (2:1). Habakkuk knew he wouldn't find an answer by accusing, screaming, or weeping. He'd have to rely on God.

This principle often strikes us as simplistic. "Just put it in Jesus' hands and it'll be all right!" we say with singsong mockery. Yet this is a solid truth emphasized throughout Scripture. Habakkuk was wrestling with issues which few people, if any, have ever understood. For all of us there come those times when we must decide to put something in God's hands and wait. If He answers in simple terms, so much the better. But His answers may take many years. And they may become terrifically complex. This is because we often have to mature in our faith and walk before we can receive His answer. God has to make us grow taller before we can reach the spices on the top shelf.

As a young Christian I fell in with a church group who believed fervently in predestination. This doctrine incensed me. I couldn't believe God could be like this—actually choosing people to be His children (rather than us choosing Him). I would go to the beach and lie down weeping. "What happened to you, Lord? I thought you were loving?" I'd find a verse that supported my side, go back to my friends, and argue. But gradually light etched its first rays in my mind and the Lord opened my heart to truths about His sovereignty, love, power, and person that I never imagined. I came to know Him in a deeper and more resplendent way than ever before. I had to grow before I could know.

Habakkuk's example is one we need to heed. Many times we, too, need to turn a concern over to God and simply wait.

TAKE TIME TO MEDITATE ON GOD'S WORD

But Habakkuk also did something else: He took time to *meditate on God's word.* He went to the guard post and kept watch to see what God would say and how he would "reply when I am reproved." That's a crucial statement. Habakkuk didn't just clamber up to the rampart, peer east, and say, "Well, guess I'll just watch the grass grow while I'm waiting." No, he meditated on the situation. He thought about every possible answer God might give. His mind went to this verse and that verse. He compared Isaiah with Jeremiah and Hosea with Job. He reviewed history. He thought about God's character. He got all tangled up inside, then found a thread leading to another idea. He tracked down that idea and then would get all tangled up again.

Meditation is a prime necessity for anyone who wants to wrestle with the great theological questions such as Habakkuk raised. As we learn to ask the Spirit questions, to talk through a truth, to follow this trail and that trail, and to get thick into it with all our heart and soul, we'll begin to probe the depths of God. We'll know Him as never before. Without meditation, we only wallow in the muck of human wisdom and speculation. But through it we catch a daring glimpse of who God is just as Moses saw Him from the cleft of the rock.

Over the years I have worked through many faith-boggling problems: free will and God's sovereignty, the baptism of the Holy Spirit, speaking in tongues, infant baptism versus believer's baptism, the inspiration of Scripture, the humanity and deity of Christ. When I first encounter such doctrines I'm often knocked about with questions, doubts, and fears.

But for several years now I've engaged in a process of memorizing whole books of the Bible. During my forty-minute drive to and from work, and on my lunch break as well as other free time, I review those books and meditate on the passages. It's startling how often a truth or idea I've never seen suddenly gleams in my mind and fills in another slot in the vast theological puzzle of life. It's thrilling to go to the Lord with a question, ask Him to provide wisdom, and then watch Him enlighten me over a period of months, even years. Each day becomes an adventure. Each new truth takes a place in my heart like a piece of armor protecting me against the terrors of Satan. I begin to feel I can fear no person on earth or anywhere else except the Lord Himself. And any fear I might have of Him becomes a daring trust that enables me to attempt anything in and through Him.

I suspect that's something of what was happening to Habakkuk. As he meditated, his fears began to dissipate. He was set free.

GOD ALWAYS ANSWERS

But as Habakkuk stood and meditated on the possibilities, God's answer came. Habakkuk knew it would come, for God is always reliable. While He may not answer as we might think, while His answer may startle or grieve or even terrify, He still answers. Always. It may be ten years down the road. But it comes. We can stand on this principle: *When we go to God with our questions, He will respond.*

God told Habakkuk to record the vision because it would not fail. He also said that the righteous man lives by faith. In other words, God assured Habakkuk that those who obey and love Him would be spared.

The five woes God pronounces in chapter two become potent judgments upon all evil everywhere—the evil perpetrated by the Hebrews and the Chaldeans, and by all men in every place. God was saying, "Be warned. I hate what you're doing. You shall not escape if you continue in your sin." A woe never came lightly. It was God's final word to hardened hearts.

GOD'S WORD BRINGS COMFORT

Though God's words to Habakkuk tell of devastation upon the land, His words are powerfully comforting. *God's word always gives hope, joy, and freedom even in the midst of hard realities.* Have you ever discovered the comfort in knowing God is the Judge of all the earth?

There's comfort first in the fact that the God who is holy and righteous is the Judge. Ultimately He will settle every dispute, every crime, every evil deed in history. Every wrong will be avenged.

There's also comfort in knowing that those who are getting away (literally) with murder now will someday face God. They will answer for their crimes. No matter how bad things look in this world, we can know God's day is coming. Every wrong will be righted.

It also means that evil persists now only because God is patient and has a plan He is presently carrying out. As Peter says, God is patient toward us, "not wishing for any to perish but for all to come to repentance" (2 Peter 3:9). God gives everyone a chance to repent.

Paul asks, "What if God, although willing to demonstrate His wrath and to make His power known, endured with much patience vessels of wrath prepared for destruction? And He did so in order that He might make known the riches of His glory upon vessels of mercy, which He prepared beforehand for glory" (Romans 9:22-23). As God lets evil run its course, He's actually thinking of you and me. He could have said in the days of Noah, "Well, this is the end." But He saw Abraham and the people of Israel. He wanted to include them in His kingdom.

Or He might have ended it all after the death of Jesus. But He saw you and me in the twentieth century and said,

"I could destroy evil now. But I love those people way up there in the twentieth century, so I'll let history run up to them. I want my kingdom to include them too."

You see, if God decided to terminate evil today, that would be the end of creation. The Lord had two choices—judge and destroy evil immediately or let it run its course, while at the same time working in its midst to fulfill the most God-glorifying and people-saving plan in history: redemption through Jesus Christ.

That's thrilling, isn't it?

HOW WE RESPOND TO THE EVIL OF OUR DAY

When we consider these things, we can look at the incredible evils that reign in our nation and world today—homosexuality, abortion, crime, revolution, terrorism, and so on—with a different perspective. Habakkuk's outlook refreshes us and reinstills that faith which is able to endure in the midst of injustice and oppression.

FEAR GOD FIRST AND FOREMOST

Habakkuk says, "Lord, I have heard the report about Thee and I fear" (3:2). Habakkuk had learned true fear of God.

That's a strange idea to many of us. We tend to think such an emotion or reaction is wrong for Christians. Love him? Yes. Obey him? Certainly. But "fear him?" It doesn't sound right. He's my Friend, my Lord, my Master, my King. Not a bully with a club.

But He's also my Judge, my Sovereign Ruler, my disciplining Father. When we grasp these aspects of His being, we begin to understand what real fear of God is. By revering and respecting God, we're enabled to love and worship Him in spirit and truth. There's awe, hope, love, and excitement all involved in our relationship with Him.

When we fear God, we don't barge into His presence like boppers at a sock hop; we don't get cute and call Him

"My buddy"; we don't flip through His word, whiz through a verse, and go merrily down the pike. No, we revere Him. His word is our starting gun. His friendship is our prized possession. His glory is Item One on our schedule of priorities. Such fear also involves dread of sin. Anyone who truly fears God will dread sin, flee sin, and fight sin; and when he sins, confess it quickly without making excuses. Fear also involves trust. When we fear God we trust Him. We look to Him for every need, every question, every concern.

Do you fear God? If you don't, do you know why you don't? There is only one reason: because you haven't seen Him as He is. When Habakkuk saw who God was, he feared. Lack of fear comes from the lack of knowledge of God.

RECOGNIZE GOD'S WISDOM

A second thought comes from Habakkuk's statement, "O Lord, revive Thy work in the midst of the years" (3:2b). He was saying, "Since this is your will, Lord, let's get on with it. Your way is the right way, the best way." Habakkuk bowed to God's wisdom. He knew God wasn't making a mistake.

Have you ever told God He's making a mistake? Not in so many words, perhaps, but by implication. Sometimes I find myself saying when evil strikes or problems explode, "Why are you letting this happen, Lord?" What we're really saying is, "Don't You know You're supposed to make me happy, Lord?"

By seeing God for who He is—all-knowing, wise, and therefore perfectly capable of running the universe without our advice—the Christian can give thanks when evil seems to have the winning edge. He knows God has everything well in hand.

That doesn't mean we shouldn't cry out against injustice. It doesn't mean we shouldn't seek to change the oppressive laws and attitudes in our midst. But we must remember that people's hearts aren't changed by the law of the land. Only the gospel can change a sinner's outlook. It's more important for us to change the lawmakers' hearts through preaching the Word than it is to change their laws. Lawmakers have an uncanny way of circumventing their own laws if their hearts aren't in it.

CRY FOR MERCY, NOT JUSTICE

Habakkuk then cried for mercy. He said, "In wrath remember mercy" (3:2). What had Habakkuk been screaming for not long ago? Judgment! Wrath! "Do something about those sinners, God!"

But what happens when we see what the holy God must do about sin? We cry for mercy! "Oh, Lord, I didn't know it was really this bad. Please forget my pleas. Be merciful." If God decides to do something about the evil in the universe tomorrow, He might not start with the Russians or the Chinese. He might start with you and me!

But our greatest joy is the knowledge of God's grace. In Jesus He extends to us forgiveness, freedom, eternal life, heaven, hope. When a sinner bows before God, admits his sin, and cries for forgiveness, God doesn't hesitate, or say, "Let me think about it." He doesn't bang his fist down and bellow, "You think a little apology like that makes everything okay?" No, He instantly applies the salvation in Christ. The sinner is cleansed. Hope is renewed. Joy is stoked.

Habakkuk had seen God. He'd seen what happens when God judges. Now he feels for those sinners. He doesn't want them to burn in hell. He longs that the God of mercy will turn them around and turn them into children of God.

WORSHIP HIM—HE IS WORTHY

Moreover, Habakkuk recognized that God was worthy. Evil wasn't really winning. Rather, a holy God of grace and love was working out an incomparable plan that led to the highest good of the universe. Habakkuk 3:3-16 is one of the great praise psalms of the Bible. Habakkuk praised God for His glory, power, justice, and majesty. He would trounce the forces of evil in a glorious panorama of triumph. He marches against evil. He tramples the nations. He wins as easily as blowing out a match. All this evil that looked so formidable and entrenched evaporates in one final blast from His lips. Habakkuk falls before this majestic Lord and worships. "O God, You are far greater than I ever imagined. It is only your patience and mercy that lets evil have its day. Forgive me, I didn't know how great you really were."

TRUST GOD REGARDLESS OF WHAT COMES

But there's one more truth: *God is worthy of our trust.* Because of all Habakkuk saw, he knew he could trust God. Everything was well under control. Though it looked bad from Habakkuk's vantage point, God knew precisely how to deal with every matter from beginning to end.

The conclusion of chapter three is a marvelous statement of faith. "Though the fig tree should not blossom, and there be no fruit on the vines, though the yield of the olive should fail, and the fields produce no food, though the flock should be cut off from the fold, and there be no cattle in the stalls, yet I will exult in the Lord, I will rejoice in the God of my salvation. The Lord God is my strength, and He has made my feet like hinds' feet, and makes me walk on my high places" (3:17-19). Habakkuk is saying, "No matter how bad it looks, no matter what goes wrong, no matter how much it looks like evil is winning—I still know the truth. It is trust in God alone that helps us stand. Therefore, I will cleave to Him."

Habakkuk understood now that he'd seen things through the wrong lenses. He saw evil getting stronger, and he figured God had gotten weaker. He saw evil trouncing the poor, and he thought God was apathetic. He saw evil enlarging and hauling everything into its maw, and he was sure God just didn't care.

But now Habakkuk had seen God as He was, is, and would be. Now he could exult. God was in charge of every detail of life. He could be trusted totally to bring it all out right. There was no reason ever to fear again.

What then did Habakkuk learn in tackling this terrible issue of evil? The most important principle of life: *Live by faith.*

This is the lesson the Lord wants to teach us all: to look to Him and His Word—not circumstances, experience, philosophy, or human wisdom.

How will God teach us that lesson? The same way He did with Habakkuk. By forcing us to wrestle with the issues of life. And when we can't find answers, by teaching us to come to Him so that He might provide insight. So be prepared. If the Lord isn't presently bringing questions, problems, difficulties, and distresses into your life, He will. It's the only way He can make us into people who think as He thinks and see as He sees.

You've heard it all before—
Sunday school and up. Every grade.
Vacation Bible school was crammed
with lessons about him.
Sermons? Two a year:
one on him and the widow; one
about Mount Carmel. You're almost bored.
You know all about it:
the prophets of Baal versus
the prophet of God.
The preachers called it, "Jehovah fights Baal,
a one-round spectacle."

The Baalies dance, scream, pray,
slash their arms, writhe about. For hours.
Even the pastor gets hot.
But the god of fire can't even cut loose
with a Blue Tip match.
Elijah taunts them: "So where's Baal?
Out getting dinner? Maybe down at the beach?
Perhaps he's on a vacation."
Elijah could get real sarcastic.
So the Baalies give up.

All the faces in the crowd shift to Elijah,
bored from Baal's blowout.
And Elijah does it up.
Gallons of water so deep
the kids want a dip.
Rocks the size of monuments.
Fresh beef.
He prays.

And zap!
A thunderbolt crashes through the blue.
The whole mountain quakes.
Water, rocks, bull vanish
like a mosquito whapped by a torch.
Not even time to snap a shot
for the Times.

The crowd is ready to cash in
their eyes
when Elijah begins hacking up
the Baal brotherhood—
a clean swipe.
Not a prophet left
with attached head and shoulders.

Then it's finished.
the prophet prays for rain, his cape flapping
in the wind. The downpour pours down.
It's Elijah's greatest moment.

Then Jezebel, the little old lady
from Samaria, fires off a memo:
"Elijah, we're going to get you for this!"
And the prophet tears for the trees—
a grizzly run off by a skunk.

"It's strange," we say.
"How can this be?"

But God understands.
He simply sends in an angel
with honeycakes, sleeping tablets,
and closed lips, and puts Elijah back together,
then gives him another job
without a dock in pay
or a demotion for a day.

That's the real miracle.

9

Elijah:

"I FEEL SO
LET DOWN"

I remember the day well. I was pastor of a church that wasn't growing. The strongest response my sermons were getting was blank stares, an occasional cough, and long sighs over a watch face.

I had gone home the previous week determined to wow them the next Sunday. I would study like I never studied. I would pray like I never prayed. Like the old black orator, I would meditate, cogitate, preponderate, and put in arousements! This coming Sunday I would show them my real stuff.

I did everything as I planned. Sunday came. And went. I staggered into our apartment door where my wife sat still recovering from her pregnancy morning sickness; she read my face instantly. I sat down and shook my head, at the point of tears or rage, whichever came first.

She said, "Was it that bad?"

I nodded.

She said, "Tell me about it."

I told her how people sat there blinking back the sleep as I preached. How they halfheartedly mumbled, "Thanks, pastor," as I stood at the door shaking their hands. How one had complained about the message being so long. I concluded, "I'm gonna quit, Val. This time I am. I can't take this any more."

She touched my arm and gave me a long hug. "I think you're a good preacher," she said.

I sighed. "Yeah, but you're supposed to." Suddenly, she got hot. She stood up, still dizzy from the morning sickness, and began telling who was who and what was what. "Has God died?" she asked. "Didn't He call you to the ministry? Is it His plan that you fail?" She ripped and roared into the greatest sermon I ever heard on why I should and would be a great pastor. She used vivid illustrations from life—mine! It had an outline of ten points—some alliterated. There was explanation, illumination, reproof, rebuke, and exhortation. I tell you, I wanted to take notes. I asked her if I could use it the next Sunday. She replied, "Get your own material!"

We both exploded with laughter. Suddenly, things didn't look so bad anymore.

I have faced the Quit Demon many times since. Often, it is because of the incredible expectations I have as I ram myself forward into a "great work for God."

The story of Elijah has a lot to say to those of us who are tempted to quit. He not only wanted to quit, he did quit. He reached what he thought was the end of the rainbow and found nothing but leftover gravy. He suffered one of the biggest letdowns in history: not a single convert after the Mount Carmel duel between God and Baal. Elijah's story provides perspective and wisdom for those of us who have watched our plans fail.

HOW WE SET OURSELVES UP FOR A CRASH

Amazing as it may seem, Elijah's depression in 1 Kings 19 was the result of several circumstances typical of people who serve God with unusual courage and zeal. Sometimes we set ourselves up for a big letdown. What helped to promote Elijah's discouragement?

TOO MUCH TIME ALONE

When we meet Elijah in 1 Kings 17, he is stepping into the pages of Scripture with a resounding boast to one of Israel's wickedest kings ever, Ahab. "As the LORD, the God of Israel lives, before whom I stand, surely there shall be neither dew nor rain these years, except by my word" (1 Kings 17:1).

Elijah was a man who identified totally with God. When he saw God's name blasphemed and scorned, he became incensed. "No one should treat God like this!" This is a tremendous quality for a Christian to possess, but it often carries with it a great weakness: Such people tend to become loners. "No one else is committed like me." Elijah spent the next three years in seclusion, an enemy of the kingdom. That was too much time alone. As a result, when everything went wrong, he lost perspective, and he didn't have any friends to fall back on to provide it.

A spiritual general needs spiritual support troops. That's one reason discouraged people need the church. It provides the hope, encouragement, and human warmth that all of us require when our own coals dim.

TOWERING PERSONAL CONFIDENCE

In his zeal, though, Elijah had to do something. He couldn't simply stand there and say, "Well, they're sinners. What do you expect?" Or, "You can't cram religion down their throats. We must be patient." No, he had to take action. "God's name must be magnified," he told himself. "These people must learn how great He is."

Elijah couldn't bear to see people continue in their lost condition. He was the kind of person who says, "Some people want a church on Main Street, but give me a rescue mission on the edge of hell." He hurt to see people live in that condition. He had to go. He had to tell them. He was willing to do anything that would wham those lost souls out of their stupor.

He decided to ask God to stop the rain. God sent him to the brook Kerith, then fed and supplied him with the little water that was left in the land.

And it didn't rain. For a month. Two months. Six months. A year.

Imagine it. Suppose you stomped down to Washington, D.C. and told the president, "You've let iniquity reign in the land. Sin is rampant. You support ungodly causes, sinful people. I'm going to do this: I'll pray that it stops raining in the United States. For as long as I pray, I swear, not one drop will fall on American soil."

Like Ahab, I'm sure the president would chuckle. "Another one of those religious nuts! We'll see."

But then it happens. It's all over the news. Headlines. "Where is so and so? $10,000 reward for anyone giving a tip that leads to his capture."

The economy is falling apart. People are starving, screaming. "Do something! Stop this man."

What confidence Elijah must have had! Nonetheless, power like that, even in the hands of a man of God, can go to your head. Something very subtle began to creep into Elijah's outlook. Some call it the "Messiah complex." I suspect Elijah began to think he was the only one who could turn Israel around. To be sure, he was praying. But the combination of his loss of perspective and his sense of power made him think he had all the answers.

EXTREMELY HIGH EXPECTATIONS

These factors led Elijah to begin formulating the "grand plan." He challenged the Baal-worshipers to demonstrate their god's power. He said to the people, "How long will you hesitate between two opinions? If the LORD is God, follow Him; but if Baal, follow him" (18:21). Then he outlined the test. All proposed and done, the people replied, "That is a good idea" (18:24).

Elijah thought if he could simply prove how great God was, everyone—including Ahab—would proclaim God

Lord and live holy ever after. I'm convinced Elijah thought the spectacle on Mount Carmel would change King Ahab's heart forever. He had thought it up for that purpose. He ran all the way to Jezreel because he wanted to see the start of "The Great Revival of 856." He was sure Ahab would stomp into the house, whip off his cloak, plunk down to his desk, and issue the order: "Anyone worshiping Baal in my kingdom will be exiled. Anyone who doesn't come to synagogue every Saturday to worship God will be horse-whipped." Elijah had it all worked out.

But when Ahab actually arrived in his chariot, Elijah sniffed the first scent of evil intent. He expected the king would say, "Hey, old boy, how did you beat me here? Well, come on in. Let's have a good chat." Instead, the king hopped out of the chariot and bounded past the prophet into the house. Ahab was terrified because he had to tell Jezebel, the one who started the whole Baal cult, what had happened. Suddenly there was a scream.

"Jezebel," Elijah thought. "He's ordered her out." Minutes later a messenger stood in front of the prophet. "The queen says this to you, prophet: 'I swear by the gods, if I don't knock your head off by tomorrow like you just did to my prophets, then let them do their worst to me, because I'm coming after you.'"

THE BIG LETDOWN

Elijah was dead tired, having just run over seventeen miles. He was shocked and confused. His heart was broken. He cried out to God, "What happened? I thought they were all going to repent."

Somewhere along the way, Elijah started running ahead of God. He was like the bloodhound out for a stroll with his master. He got so excited about all the wild scents, he forgot to stick close by. Suddenly, he found himself lost. When the darkness closed in, he panicked. That's why Elijah ran into the wilderness. In the midst of all the monumental demonstrations of God's power, he lost sight of the God behind the power.

WHY GOD SOMETIMES GOES ALONG WITH OUR PLANS

Of course, there's a problem here. If what I'm saying is true, why did God do the miracle on Mount Carmel? Certainly, if we're going to make a biblical principle out of this, we'd better be sure we're correct.

There are many reasons God might have gone along with Elijah's scheme. Elijah may have wanted a revival, but perhaps God had other plans. Signs from God are meant not only to convert, but also to condemn.

It's interesting to note that there's no mention of God telling Elijah to do the Mount Carmel demonstration. All the Lord said was, "Go, show yourself to Ahab, and I will send rain on the face of the earth" (1 Kings 18:1). Furthermore, there's no indication that anyone was converted through this miracle. It appears that the seven thousand who remained true to God were there all along. It would appear Elijah was more interested in the *coup d'etat*; the showdown was arranged apart from the counsel and direction of God.

Then why did God send the thunderbolt? I believe it's because He's gracious, He loved Elijah, and didn't want His prophet looking like a fool. This is an important truth, for it explains why God sometimes seems to bless great human schemes that lead nowhere. God gives us freedom to try things, to learn, to grow, to develop on our own terms. He doesn't roll us out on wax paper, take His giant cookie cutter, and cut us out—presto! Perfect pictures of Jesus!

Whenever a Christian lets his high expectations run away with him, he's in deep water that can result in drowning. Fortunately we have a Lord who will not let us drown, even though we may have to cough up a lot of brine in the process.

DEALING WITH A LETDOWN

At that point, the Lord had one depressed prophet on His hands. He'd run into the wilderness, plunked down beneath a juniper tree, and requested to die. How did God get His man moving again? Understanding that will help us successfully and maturely deal with those occasions when we suffer a letdown.

GET REST AND RELAXATION

A discouraged saint often needs physical encouragement as well as spiritual inspiration. The first thing God did was give Elijah food and rest. It's an amazingly simple response. The Lord didn't give Elijah a lecture or refer to a Bible verse. No, He let Elijah say his piece, "It is enough; now, O LORD, take my life, for I am not better than my fathers" (19:4). Then He put him to sleep, and then sent an angel to provide food. And what food it was. Elijah lived off those two meals for forty days.

Isn't that beautiful? Giving advice is often the least effective way to deal with such a problem. What discouraged people need is TLC, not chapter and verse.

My wife always astounds me in this respect. When I clunk home, beaten from a day of screaming customers and endless difficulties, my two-year-old daughter will hurtle up to me demanding a carry and a roll on the floor. But my wife often takes one look at me, picks up Nicole, and tells me, "Why don't you go lay down? I'll bring you some ice water." After a little rest, I'm ready for a carry and a roll.

TAKE TIME TO THINK AND REEVALUATE

After two stints of sleep and food, Elijah got up. He began wandering in the direction of Horeb (Mount Sinai), a journey of at least three hundred miles. It took him forty days because of his state of mind. During that time, Elijah began asking questions, reevaluating. God gave him time to think, to work through some of the confusion and frustration.

Such therapy is critical to a discouraged saint. To be sure, we need to get squarely back upon the word of God. But we must do that on our own terms and timing. The Lord never forces us to think as He thinks, though this is His ultimate goal. He wants us to come to our conclusions freely and voluntarily.

A discouraged person needs time to think, to get those steamrolling feelings focused, to see clearly what they are.

ADMIT YOUR FEELINGS TO GOD

Nonetheless, Elijah's conclusions led him not to hope but to greater discouragement, as often happens if someone remains alone during a period of darkness. When Elijah reached Horeb and sat down by the cave, God spoke to him for the first time since before the Mount Carmel episode. God asked him what he was doing there. Elijah's answer flames with bitterness and resentment: "I have been very zealous for the LORD, the God of hosts; for the sons of Israel have forsaken Thy covenant, torn down Thine altars and killed Thy prophets with the sword. And I alone am left; and they seek my life, to take it away" (19:10). That's why he was in the cave. He told himself, "Maybe I'll be safe here—since God can't protect me."

Clearly, Elijah felt he'd given God his best, and God had reneged. God simply hadn't turned out the way Elijah figured.

Have you ever found yourself in that mindset? You start a Sunday school class sure that God will bless. Then it fizzles. Suddenly you think the Lord has evaporated from the universe. Or you get married and after a few years things start to get tough. You come close to divorce. You ask, "Lord, what's happened? Why aren't you working this out?"

When things don't turn out the way we thought, we often blame God. But it's better to admit to the Lord we feel that way, than it is to hide our feelings and pretend everything is fine. Hiding our feelings leads only to deeper discouragement. God knows our hearts. But He wants us to cease trying to hide anything from Him. Only an open and honest relationship with Him is of value.

I recall when I first began to honestly share my feelings with my wife, after thinking for a long time that I should hide my self-doubt, fear, anger, and discouragement from her. I had often walked in the door with a long face, and when she'd ask, "What's wrong?" I'd give the typical male reply: "Oh, nothing." Sometimes it would take her days to drag it out of me. If I was upset about something between us, I'd pretend I wasn't.

But as we've learned to share our feelings honestly and openly, a freshness, intimacy, and depth comes into the relationship that is precious beyond description. That's the same kind of relationship the Lord wants with us. If you're of that stripe, cease trying to pretend you're happy and confident when you're really discouraged. Go to the Lord and pour out your heart, expecting that He understands and can do something to change either the situation or you.

GET A FRESH LOOK AT WHO GOD IS

God took another step with Elijah once his feelings were in the open. He told Elijah to stand out on the mountain before Him, for He was passing by. First there was a wind so powerful the mountains were torn. But God wasn't in that wind. Next there was an earthquake. The ground shook. Elijah crouched. The shaking stopped. But God wasn't in the earthquake either. After that there was fire, a cyclone of flames. Elijah reeled from the heat. Still, God was absent.

Finally, sudden silence. An absolute stillness. Elijah must have craned his neck, blinking his eyes to see what was next. And then he heard "a sound of a gentle blowing." Covering his face with his mantle, Elijah "went out and stood in the entrance of the cave. And behold, a voice came to him . . ." (19:13). What had God been showing Elijah? There are different interpretations, but what I see is this: God was telling him, "Elijah, you've wanted to see great things happen. You've been witness to spectacular displays of my power—stopping the rain, filling a widow's pot of flour, raising the dead, and now a thunderbolt out of heaven proving once for all that Baal is nonexistent. You've had all these grandiose dreams of a revival, of the whole nation turning back to me, of the king repenting. But you've got to understand—I don't usually manifest Myself in the spectacular, in monumental displays of power. They just don't accomplish much. Elijah, you've got to understand, it's the heart I'm after. And you don't get to the heart by putting on a show."

Elijah needed a fresh understanding of God. He'd been on his own for three years. Perhaps he hadn't even had the Scriptures to study. He'd lost sight of who God was.

I believe most discouragement is overcome when we immerse ourselves in scriptural truths of who God is and what He is doing in our world. Ask yourself, "What am I assuming God promises to do that He really doesn't promise? What false views am I believing about God?" When we've got His true character deeply etched in our being, we'll not only discover uplifting encouragement and hope, but Satan and the circumstances of life will find it difficult to break us ever again.

SUBMIT TO GOD'S WILL

At that point, though, Elijah remained discouraged. Just knowing the truth about God isn't a cure-all. God had to give him several jobs to perform: to anoint two kings, one over Aram and one over Israel; and to anoint another prophet in his place, Elisha, in order to get him moving out of the darkness and into the light. These people would provide the security Elijah needed. It also gave him something to do, to get his mind off all that had happened. From God's point of view, Elijah needed to get back on course.

Imagine being involved in a battle, and your commander gives you a message for the soldiers on the front line. They've given up and are ready to surrender. The message is simple: "I'm with you. Don't surrender. We're bringing in the artillery. Hang tough."

At first you're pleased. But as you run along, you get worried. "What if they don't believe it?" The more you look at the little note in your hand, the more you begin to feel it will accomplish nothing.

Then a new idea pops into your head. "What those guys need is a real jolt. Why not do a fireworks show that writes the message in the sky? That'll convince them." You stop running with the simple message, gather together a tremendous fireworks display, set it all up, then detonate it. When it's all over, you scurry to the group anxious to see them fighting with spirit and joy.

But what do you find? A bunch of scared men quivering in the bushes. You're so disgusted, you stomp off in anger. And then the soldiers begin shooting at you! You run for the hills, discouraged and broken.

Many Christians are like that messenger. They look at God's plans—the Bible—and think, "This won't work." So they cook up some marvelous display like Elijah did on Mount Carmel. In the process, they wear themselves out with anxiety about the results. When things don't happen the way they hope, they're angry.

The message for these people is this: "Quit dreaming up all this show business and start doing the simple things outlined in the Book." God hasn't made it difficult to know His will. He tells us to preach the Word. Pray. Share the faith. Love one another. Confront sin. Give. Stand firm.

Satan's greatest strategy is veering us off the simple path and onto "Glory Road." That's the one with lots of neon lights, fireworks, people swaying in the wind, and giggles in the night. But after the initial shot of fun, Glory Road gets very discouraging because it never goes anywhere. When we stand on the simple premises and promises of God's word, He assures us, "He who began a good work in you will perfect it until the day of Christ Jesus" (Philippians 1:6).

GET WITH GOD'S PEOPLE

Finally God said, "Yet I will leave 7,000 in Israel, all the knees that have not bowed to Baal and every mouth that has not kissed him" (1 Kings 19:18). After all the unbelievers were eliminated, there would still be 7,000 left—humble, holy people committed to the Lord. Elijah would no longer be alone.

Christians who try to go it alone inevitably end up worn and weary, ready to put themselves down the sump pump. But the Lord wants us to get together. We're a body. We can't do without one another. Elijah needed to know not only that he wasn't the only one, but that the others would love and support him as he jogged along.

When it was all over, what I see is a man who has mellowed. Elijah's no longer determined to make God perform his schemes. He's content. He's willing to say, "Thy will be done, Lord. I'll let you do as you please." He knows it doesn't all rest on him.

Have you come to that place? It's an important juncture in the Christian walk. "I rest in you, Lord," is the confession of a person settled on the Rock. It's not that you're not trying, not that you never put together another plan or dream; but you've come to the place where all that matters is walking with Jesus. He's with you and that's enough.

After two years in seminary I was stricken with a harrowing, biochemical depression. I went to doctors, had all kinds of tests, memorized hordes of Bible verses, and prayed daily like a man under the waves for the last time. When I thought I might actually commit suicide, I asked my doctor to put me in the hospital.

The depression was discouraging enough. But I felt as though all the grand plans I had in going to seminary were dashed. I felt God had let me down.

I was in the hospital for a month. Many seminary friends came to visit and talk. But there was one who stood out, a classmate named Russ. I hadn't known him well, but he made the hour drive to the hospital once each week. As we sat and talked, I brought up multitudes of questions. "Why was God doing this to me? Would I ever graduate? Could I ever serve God again?" Russ nodded with compassion, but he didn't have any answers.

One day he came into my room, sat down, and said, "You know, two years ago when I first came to seminary, I wouldn't have been out here visiting someone like you. To my shame, I have to say I wouldn't have cared. But I want you to know the reason I'm here is because I do care."

He pulled out a little Matchbox truck and set it on the telephone table. He said, "I know it's not much, but it's a little hope-starter. Every time you get really down, I want you to look at that truck and imagine you and me and Jesus just driving down the road, praying and singing and going where Jesus wants us to go. Will you do that?"

I nodded.

He said, "I wish I could tell you why this is happening to you, Mark. But I want you to know I love you. I'm in this with you."

I couldn't say anything, but his kindness changed my life. I was still horribly depressed. Still confused. But somehow, I sensed that through Russ God was saying to me, "Mark, you don't understand what's going on. But I want you to know, I'm with you. We're going to see this thing through. I have all your high hopes in my heart, and I've got plans so wonderful you can't even imagine them. For now, just trust Me and follow Me. I love you."

You know, I still have that truck. Every now and then, I pick it up. And remember. I wonder if Elijah didn't think the same things every time he remembered his cave on Horeb?

All my life I've wanted to see
God do something big.
Like the parting of the Red Sea.
Riiiiiiip! Walls of water
swirling above you like cliffs.
Or Jericho. God banged down
His fist and splat, the city was flat.

Sometimes I can picture it.
Me standing up and preaching.
Five thousand converted!
Me in front of the firing squad.
I pray. Suddenly a lightning bolt
cracks through. Not a shot fired.
Just cinders where the soldiers stood.
Me writing a book.
Two million copies sold.

It'd be wonderful, wouldn't it?
I mean, for me that is.

Of course, I suppose for you it might not be
so great. But what if God did the same thing
in you, in all of us?
And what if we all prayed together
that the whole world would see
how great He is through us?

I'm game.
Are you?

10

Gideon:

"DO SOMETHING BIG, LORD"

Do you ever dream of sharing Christ before a crowd of twenty thousand? Or discipling young men who turn into evangelists, pastors, and disciplers? Or making millions of dollars through your business to pour into missions? Perhaps you'd like to start a businessmen's Bible study that cuts a swath for Christ in your community.

Most of us have great dreams as Christians. Anyone who walks with Jesus for long has to catch the vision. "Make disciples of all nations." Go "to the ends of the earth." God is able to do "exceeding abundantly beyond all that we ask or think." Such words inflame.

But after looking at Elijah and how his dreams crashed, we have to wonder. What if my dreams aren't on God's agenda? What if I get out so far ahead of the Lord I run right off a cliff? Christians sometimes come out of their dream chambers with their hopes planted firmly in midair. Like Elijah, their great expectations will end in smithereens.

Is it legitimate to dream such dreams? Or are we kidding ourselves? Is our God a God of the small instead of the grand, the little instead of the big, the subtle instead of the spectacular? Can we ever expect Him to do great things in us and through us in our generation?

When I became a Christian in August 1972, I hatched such a dream. I wanted the Lord to use me in leading ten thousand souls to himself. At the time, it looked tremendous. I was energized. I prayed about it daily.

When I became a pastor, I came up with the idea of making twenty-five thousand disciples in ten years. I worked it out on paper. All I had to do was disciple one person for six months, and at the end of that time get him to do the same, while I took on one more disciple. If each person followed through on the process, we'd have our twenty-five thousand disciples by the tenth year. The thought supercharged me. I put together reams of handouts to teach them straight theology.

Of course, it hasn't happened that way. But I still dream about it. In fact, I've decided such goals are too small. I've asked the Lord to up the figures to ten million.

Am I crazy? Is this folly?

Of course, if our reasons for pursuing such goals is glorification of self, personal fame and fortune or some other form of self-gain, we're not only deluded, but caught in the snare of Satan. But what of those who have such ambitions for the Lord's sake? What about the fellow whose only concern is that the world know how great God is? Is it wrong for such a person to want to accomplish great things in the name of Jesus?

There is one fellow in Scripture whose dreams excite me to no end: Gideon. He was a dreamer whose exploits in the name of God provide fantastic insight for those who dream big dreams.

A PORTRAIT OF A DREAMER

Most of us probably have some picture of what a person is like who "thinks big." He's the kind of Christian who rouses people up and gets things clicking. He has an infectious enthusiasm. Confident, he will try anything for God. Like Caleb he shouts, "Give me that mountain!" and then strides up the face of it like a matador into the bullring.

Gideon knocks that mold to pieces. He was no tough type who feared nothing and no one. His wasn't some kind of cheerleader who rah-rahed his way to glory. When we first see him in Judges 6, he's beating out a handful of wheat in a winepress. The Midianites have ravaged Israel weekly, stealing their crops and burning their homes. They swarm in like locusts, devour the land, then spring on to other devastations.

When the angel of God, an Old Testament appearance of Jesus Christ, comes to Gideon, Gideon reveals two traits common to true dreamers for God. Gideon says, "O my lord, if the LORD is with us, why then has all this happened to us? And where are all His miracles which our fathers told us about, saying, 'Did not the LORD bring us up from Egypt?' But now the LORD has abandoned us and given us into the hand of Midian" (Judges 6:13).

EXCITEMENT ABOUT THE EXPLOITS OF THE PAST

Gideon grew up in an age following the conquest of Canaan. Though Joshua had marched around Jericho over two centuries previous, Gideon knew the great stories. His grandpa and father told him about Abraham, Isaac, Jacob, Moses, and Joshua. Can you see Gideon listening, with chills buzzing down his back? His eyes widen as they speak of Abraham defeating the ten kings. He prays when they reminisce of Deborah and Barak annihilating Jabin, "Oh, Lord, do it again!" Those stories thrilled Gideon. He wanted to hear them over and over. He wanted to see them happen in his lifetime.

That's a dreamer. When he reads about David and Goliath, he thinks of the hulking atheist he'd like to claim for Jesus. When he sees Isaiah in God's throneroom, high and lifted up, he prays, "Oh, that I might have such an understanding of you, Lord."

A LONGING TO SEE GOD GLORIFIED TODAY

But those stories also caused Gideon to question, "If God was like that then, why isn't He doing those things now? Why are our people defeated? Why is the temple empty?" Gideon burned to see something big, something so incredible only God could have done it.

Every time a dreamer studies Scripture, he compares it to today. He wants to know, "Where are today's great revivals? Why aren't three thousand converted today after one sermon? Where are all the bold saints who can face the lions with bowed heads and trusting hearts?" It's not that he's critical of God. It's not even that he wants to see the sensational—miracles and the like. But he longs for a fresh outpouring of power. He wants to see sin vanquished, holiness pursued, and love offered. Clearly Gideon had strong notions about what happens when God is with us.

Are you such a dreamer?

It's more than simply wishing. It's a longing, an ache. A dreamer tells himself, "God is so great and no one seems to know it. Oh, that all people might see how wonderful the Lord is!"

WHAT'S HAPPENED TO THE MIRACULOUS?

We don't often see such dreams coming true today. As one man said to me, "You'd think God had up and died, the way things don't happen around here." What prevents God from doing great deeds in our midst? Gideon's story offers three reasons.

Sin. The people of Israel had sinned, were sinning, and would continue in sin if God didn't send the Midianites. One reason God wasn't blessing was because God was disciplining. He used the Midianites as a wedge to drive them away from sin and back to Himself.

When the church doesn't grow or life is a constant struggle, we should ask, "Is God disciplining us? Have we sinned?" We must examine ourselves. However, Scripture never teaches that just because we're Christians we should win the beauty contest or be All-Pro or have the biggest church or zip right up the stock exchange. Defeat isn't always spelled S-I-N. And victory is no sure indication of God's favor.

Lack of faith. That uncovers a second reason God doesn't do great things in some places: because no one has the faith to attempt such deeds. That was precisely why the angel had come to Gideon—to get him in motion so that some great things could happen.

The Lord told Gideon, "Go in this your strength and deliver Israel from the hand of Midian. Have I not sent you?" (Judges 6:14). He didn't answer any of Gideon's questions. He simply sent him. How could he explain anyway? Gideon wouldn't understand or else he'd simply argue with him.

If you hope for great works of God in your place of service, don't look back and bemoan the past. God says, "The past is forgiven. Let's start now. Are you with me?" Just as we needn't rest on our laurels, neither should we bury ourselves under our mistakes. We can always start anew with the Lord today. "Today if you hear his voice, do not harden your hearts" (Hebrews 4:7). What matters is whether we'll put our faith in Him *now* and follow Him *now*.

The minnow mentality. Still, there's another problem that often keeps us from reaching our dreams. Gideon himself brings it out in verse fifteen. "O LORD, how shall I deliver Israel? Behold, my family is the least in Manasseh, and I am the youngest in my father's house" (6:15). Gideon felt like a minnow in a sea of sharks. This mentality is what halts most dreamers before they even attempt anything. When God actually tells us to do something—start that class or go to that neighbor—we balk. "I don't know enough!" "I've never done anything like that before."

Again, God has the answer. He told Gideon, "Surely I will be with you, and you will defeat Midian as one man." He gave Gideon assurance that He was on his side. "One plus God is a majority."

THE PROCESS OF ATTEMPTING A GREAT WORK FOR GOD

Once Gideon was prepared to go in God's name and accomplish the great deeds God had prepared, there was still a process he had to go through. This process reflects important guidelines for bringing about the movement of the Spirit in our generation.

FOLLOW GOD'S DIRECTIONS

The trouble most of us have in forging ahead with our plans is that we improvise with God's directions. Dreamers tend to be creative, imaginative people. They're always whipping up a batch of new ideas they want to try on their disciples. They're sure such ideas will rouse their disciples into a holy frenzy. Too often, though, they become creative in the wrong areas.

What I mean, for instance, is that we will take a simple directive from God such as, "Preach the word; be ready in season and out of season; reprove, rebuke, exhort" (2 Timothy 4:2) and add our own variations. Instead of preaching the Word, we change God's directive to, "Preach the findings of modern psychology; excite, challenge, up-lift." Or we go in another direction: "Preach what you happen to be interested in at the moment; be profound, captivating, motivating." Others turn it this way: "Preach what you think the people will like; make 'em laugh, make 'em cry, make 'em feel religious."

God has given us marvelous latitude to be creative within His command. We can outline our messages any way we want. We can use alliteration, rhyme, or other devices. We can dream up our own analogies and illustrations, and even razzle and dazzle our folks with a dramatic monologue or a striking object lesson. But we're to preach the Word—not our own opinions or those of the latest self-help artist.

We must learn to be creative where God allows creativity, and obedient where God has given us specific instructions. God's directions must be followed—no matter what.

This is precisely what we find in Gideon's situation. Once Gideon became convinced God was with him, God gave him his first job. It was a small one compared with what would come later, but it was a vast undertaking for a minnow. God sent him to tear down his father's idols, then build a new altar, and offer a bull to God using the wood of the idol as kindling.

Notice the simplicity of God's directions. He lays it out step by step. "Do this and you'll succeed, Gideon." Gideon could carry out the orders when and with whom he wanted.

God's word is astonishingly simple. We make it complex by trying to find the odd interpretation that frees us from having to do what He says. But in actuality, His simple commands are a source of security rather than fear. We can't make any mistake about what He wants; we can know if we're pleasing Him.

GOD IS ALWAYS FAITHFUL

When people saw what Gideon had done the next morning, they wanted to sacrifice him. But Gideon's father answered them with perfect logic: "Look, if Baal is really a god, then he'll get Gideon. You don't need to go after him." That satisfied them and Gideon even received a new nickname: "Jerubbaal," which means "Let Baal contend with him."

When we seek to do a work for God and people oppose us, God Himself will defend us. He may put our enemies to shame with a deft shot of logic or something else. But He won't let them destroy us if He's got bigger plans ahead.

I remember reading of a tribe in Africa who threatened a missionary daily with death. But every night as they crept through the trees to slay him, they became afraid. When tribesmen later were converted, they asked the missionary, "Who were the shining ones who protected you each night when we came to kill you?" The missionary didn't know. But obviously God had sent His angels to protect him just as Elisha and Gehazi were protected in Dothan (2 Kings 6).

EXPECT THAT GOD WILL TEST YOU

God gave Gideon that first job of destroying the idols as a test. Would Gideon prove faithful to the command? Or would he go his own way? God needed someone loyal to Him to lead the people. The episode with the idols demonstrated both. Gideon proved his boldness and leadership by taking initiative and defying evil. He also passed his first major test in God's classroom by doing as he was told.

Anyone who seeks to achieve great things for Jesus will be tested. God cannot offer us great tasks if we prove faithless in little ones. A dreamer must reckon with the fact that God doesn't offer gold to fools, nor does He give a throne (or a pulpit) to an imposter. Notice that the job God gave Gideon was what I'd call a "faith-sized" task—one that stretched him but didn't break him. By testing and proving him in the smaller task, God prepared Gideon for the larger one.

John Knox cried to God, "Give me Scotland or I die." So God gave him a little pulpit. In a short time, though, God gave him thunder for the whole land.

If any of us wants to dream big dreams for God, we must get on with the work in the little places or we'll never reach the big places. What small task has God given you now? Have you proven faithful? Why should God give you more disciples if you're slack with the ones you have? Why should He send you ten students if you're not preparing well for your class of five? Solomon said, "Do you see a man skilled in his work? He will stand before kings; he will not stand before obscure men" (Proverbs 22:29). If we strive for skill now in the little things, we'll soon find the Lord entrusting the riches to our care.

LEARN TO RELY ON THE POWER OF THE SPIRIT

No one can do anything apart from God's personal power. After Gideon was tested, the "Spirit of the Lord came upon him." This was a special anointing of the power and presence of God for a special time. It was temporary.

It's different from the indwelling of the Spirit as we know it in the New Testament. All Christians have God's Spirit within them (Romans 8:9). The difference is that we possess the Spirit permanently.

But that's the only difference.

Did you get that? *The same Spirit that came upon Gideon for that short time dwells in us all the time.* We not only have the same resource Gideon did, but we have Him forever.

There's only one thing that prevents the Spirit from filling anyone: disobedience. Disobedience includes any refusal to obey what we know God says. The question is, What teachings, truths, or promises have you come across that you're ignoring or disobeying?

This is what happens to me. I come across a verse like, "Husbands, love your wives as Christ loved the church." I say, "That's a nice verse. I think I'll memorize it." I memorize it. Then one day I'm sitting in the living room and my wife says, "Will you rub my back?"

Oh, how I hate rubbing backs. I reply, "Can't I do it later?"

She says, "Please."

I grit my teeth and start rubbing. Then God raps me with a question: "Is that loving your wife as Christ loved the church?"

I whine, "But, Lord, my fingers hurt and it takes so long and I need to read the newspaper and I'm tired and . . . ."

"Is that the way Jesus loved you?"

Now I'm faced with the real issue. Will I obey gladly, thank Him for the opportunity, and give her the best rubdown in the East? Or will I grit my teeth and obey outwardly, but scream inside, "I'll do it this time, but this is the last one for a week!" Which way is real obedience? Both look good outwardly (though she does notice that my face is crimson). But God looks on the heart.

The reason so few Christians ever experience the filling of the Spirit is not because we don't obey God outwardly. No, it's because there's no inward obedience, no submission, no gladness in serving God.

As Gideon fed on God and His gifts, the Lord empowered him. God can do the same thing in us.

GO TO GOD WITH YOUR DOUBTS

But that doesn't mean we won't waver, or doubt, or suffer anxiety. After Gideon called the people, sent messengers through the land, laid down the challenge, and formulated his plan, he was ready for the great work of his life. But suddenly doubt struck. "What if everyone really does follow me? What if I get out there in the midst of battle and God deserts me?" Always, always, when we set out upon a great work for God, there will be hesitation. Satan plants seeds of doubt. The world starts to look awesome. And our own flesh begins telling us how weak we are. Rather than wrestle with our doubts, we need to go to God with them; He will provide the insight, power, and resources necessary to overcome them.

Gideon decided one last time to make sure before he began this enterprise. He laid out a fleece. We all know the story. As a result, people through the ages have followed Gideon's example and "laid out fleeces" to confirm God's will. Though it's a side issue, we should ask, Is such a practice necessary?

No. Fleeces are extremely dangerous—because they are so easily faked and coincidental. If we're going to "put out a fleece," then at least lay out one that only God could do. We shouldn't say, "If the phone rings in the next five minutes, then I know you want me to do this." Or, "If Joe comes up to me in church today, then I'll know for sure." What we pray should be something like, "If all the grass on my lawn turns scarlet in the next five minutes, then God is in it."

A fleece will not keep us in God's work, nor will lack of a fleece get us out. If we want to serve the Lord, let's do so out of conviction and faith, not because of some gimmick that occurred way back when.

God understands our hesitation and fear. As with Gideon, He often gives us that last whack to push us through the door on a work we're just not sure about.

If you long to do a great work for God but simply aren't sure He's in it with you, first consult the Scriptures. If what you want to do is sanctioned by the Lord, plough ahead. God always honors those who honor his Word. If you need further assurance and confirmation, simply ask Him to give you the wisdom you need. He'll provide. On the other hand, if you're wondering whether He wants you to start a ministry of worshipful bellydancing or some such thing (don't laugh, I've heard such testimonies on TV!), you'll find no support either from the Scriptures or a fleece or anything else.

LET GOD LEAD IN THE CHOICE OF HELPERS

At this point, it's easy to sprint off eager to get going on the job at hand, but that opens us up to satanic interference and attack. If we use poor judgment, we may choose the wrong people to come along with us. That could wreck the whole adventure before it even starts. That was why God took Gideon through a selection process. When thirty-two thousand people showed up after Gideon gave the call, who wouldn't have cheered? If our church decides to start an evangelism program and fifty percent of the people sign up, what could be better?

For Gideon, thirty-two thousand was quite an army. It would be too easy to make the mistake of thinking they'd won the battle on their own. So God told him to cut down the numbers by sending anyone who was afraid away.

What if we did that in our churches? "Hey, anybody who was wrangled into this and really doesn't want to teach Sunday school (or be on this committee), feel free to leave." How many would we have left? Probably the kind of teachers that would turn a church around.

But God still wasn't satisfied. He cut the numbers further by telling Gideon to watch the men as they drank. The ones who laid their faces right down in the water were rejected. But those who scooped the water and lapped it from their palms were the right choices. And suddenly, there were only three hundred left. Just enough to get the job done without anyone thinking they did it on their own.

Why did God eliminate so many willing people? One reason was to force Gideon to rely on God. Any time a job is necessary in the kingdom of God, people are tempted to get moving. "Time is running out," we cry. "If we don't move now, all is lost." We get out our organizational charts, plot the growth curve, assign the committees, work out the chain of command, and steam ahead. But in a situation like this, when Gideon knew he was now so outnumbered there was no hope of victory, he had to rely on God. "If you don't do it, Lord, we're fried."

Another important reason was that God got the glory. What do people say when a church spurts with growth, moves from five families to five hundred in two years, and the man behind it is this slick handsome guy with a sharp message? "The man's brilliant!" "What an organizer." "What a dynamic speaker." But what do we call him when he's this runt of a guy who's rather dull to listen to, is always getting into trouble, talks constantly about how great Jesus is, and ends up beheaded? "The apostle Paul." When Paul came to town no one thought anything except that God must have done it.

But there's an even more important reason from a human perspective. God wanted to teach these people to obey Him even when it looked impossible. Three hundred men against 135,000? Even with modern hand grenades, machine guns, and mortars it would be difficult. But these men were armed only with clay pitchers, sticks, torches, and trumpets.

This is still another brand of obedience—obedience even when it looks downright preposterous.

Have you ever thought how often God commands us to do things which, by the world's standards, are foolish, even ludicrous? God says, "Love your enemies and pray for those who persecute you" (Matthew 5:44). The world replies, "Beat 'em up." God says, "Ask and it shall be given to you" (Matthew 7:7). The world snickers. "No way. Rather, go for your own gusto!"

While working in a restaurant in Vermont, I tried repeatedly to witness to my fellow workers. Some were receptive, some indifferent. But one was malicious, even evil. Several times she took great pleasure in using God's name for everything but worship in my presence just to get me angry. Frankly, I wrote her off. "No way, Lord. Not even you could convert this one."

One day I was reading Hal Lindsey's book, *Satan Is Alive and Well on Planet Earth,* and I came upon a passage that described demon possession. Suddenly, the lights came on. That very moment, I felt a strange urge to find this worker and tell her she was in great danger and had to trust Jesus. I almost laughed. "You can forget that, Lord. She'll bite my nose off." But the urge pressed even more firmly.

I went down to her room, knocked, and looked in. No one home. I shrugged and was about to go, when suddenly she appeared. I asked her if we could talk. She snickered. Then I told her what I'd been reading about demons and thought she might have one! Her face contorted, but I blurted out, "You must call on the Lord right now—you need help! You've alienated every one here. Pray now, or you can't be sure what will happen." I was quaking.

But suddenly she closed her eyes and screeched, "Jesus, help me! I need you."

I don't know whether this was a true case of demon possession, but I know what happened after that. She began searching the Scriptures, praying, attending a little group I led, and bubbled over with a new joy and kindness never seen before.

Sometimes what looks impossible to us is easy for the Lord, if we'll only obey.

SPEND TIME WITH GOD TO DEVELOP YOUR STRATEGY

Finally, for Gideon, everything was in order. God even gave him one last assurance by sending him down to the Midianite camp to overhear a prophetic dream by one of the enemy soldiers. God wanted his man to proceed boldly.

It was then that Gideon divulged his battle plan. The three hundred men were divided into three groups. Each man had a trumpet and a pitcher with a torch in it. When it turned pitch dark, the men spread out in a circle about the Midianite camp. Then Gideon blew on his trumpet. Immediately, the other men broke their pitchers and trumpeted away.

The instant it happened, Midian was thrown into confusion. Encircled and in the dark, the soldiers jumped up and began flailing away at everything that moved. At the same time, God supernaturally created such pandemonium that soon 120,000 swordsmen of Midian were dead.

Such strategy is critical to success in bringing off a great work for God. All the greats of the Bible formulated bold and decisive strategies in order to accomplish their goals. The question is, where did Gideon get this strategy? Was he some master tactician or did God give it to him or did he simply dream it up and God worked it through?

Strangely, the text gives no indication of how Gideon arrived at this battle plan. But let's speculate about it.

Several factors pinpoint possible reasons for Gideon's monumental finesse.

First, notice that Gideon had exercised caution every step of the way. At each juncture he asked for and received confirmation of God's leading. That indicates something important: Gideon had an ability to wait on God. What I think Gideon had done was to meditate, plan, look at it this way and that way. In the process, God opened up his mind to possibilities he'd never have thought of on his own. It's this process of talking with God and reflecting on his truth that leads to the great ideas that win battles and shake our world. Flashes of insight come only when we walk in the Light.

Second, Gideon had been worshiping God all along. That's also important, because it's in the midst of worship that we begin to think like God. And thinking like God leads to great deeds with God. Do you want to accomplish great things with and for Jesus? Then spend time with Him—meditating, communing, and worshiping. There is no other way to develop the mind of Christ that leads to deeds like Christ's."

FOR BIG DREAMERS ONLY

As I look at Gideon through all this, I see a young man who longed for a day when Israel would be free. Never again would the Midianites invade and plunder the land. He cried out to God for a people who would stand with him and love God. Above all, he burned to see God do the wondrous deeds of old, like he had heard from his grandfathers. Gideon wanted to see everything God could do.

When I reflect on some of my biggest dreams and ambitions I think of Ephesians 3:20—"Now to him who is able to do exceeding abundantly beyond all that we could ask or think." Those words "exceeding abundantly" in Greek are *hyper-ek-perissos*, a superlative from the root *perissos*. That word is used in John 10:10—"I came that they might have life and have it more *abundantly.*" It means, "profuse, going beyond what is necessary."

In the form *ek-perissos*, the word is used only once in Scripture, in Mark 14:31—Peter kept saying *insistently,* 'Even if I have to die with you, I will not deny you.'" It means "going far, far beyond what's necessary." Peter kept saying it over and over, more emphatically each time.

Now you can better sense the drama of Paul's use of the form *hyper-ek-perissos*. For with "hyper," it means even greater excess and abundance "beyond what is necessary." Think again of the verse: "Now to Him who is able to do hyper-abundantly beyond all that you can ask or think." Do you see the idea? We can't even ask enough from God. We can't even begin to think of all He can and will do!

As far as I'm concerned all my dreams above are merely playthings. We haven't seen anything from the Lord yet!

HOW CAN IT HAPPEN?

Can it happen, then?

Yes.

But how?

There's a simple way. All we have to do is what Gideon did. First, believe everything God says. Second, do it. Obey.

Do you get the picture? You take everything you now know that God commands and teaches, and you obey it. Everything. Whatever He says, do. Even if you don't understand why. Even if it's hard. Even if it means persecution and pain. Even if everyone laughs at you—even other Christians.

Every day learn more from His word and apply more. When you fail to obey, confess it and go on.

"But what if God doesn't do those incredible things you dream of? What if we just plod along in life and never realize those dreams?"

How God uses us in this world is His choice. Some— like Martin Luther and Billy Graham—He has employed in monumental, visible ways. But others accomplished great deeds in hidden, subtle ways. It will all be revealed at the judgment seat of Christ.

I often think of it as Shadrach, Meshach, and Abednego did. Remember how Nebuchadnezzar commanded them to worship his golden image and they refused? He threatened to put them in the fiery furnace. He said, "What god is there who can deliver you out of my hands?" (Daniel 3:15).

The three faithful men replied, "O Nebuchadnezzar, we do not need to give you an answer concerning this. If it be so, our God whom we serve is able to deliver us from the furnace of blazing fire; and He will deliver us out of your hand, O king. But even if He does not, let it be known to you, O king, that we are not going to serve your gods or worship the golden image that you have set up" (Daniel 3:16-18).

What magnificent obedience! These men were saying, "We can't be responsible for what God does. We can be responsible only for our obedience. We must obey Him regardless of what He chooses to do." We must obey God out of love, worship, respect, and fear whether he chooses to use us as billboards or doormats. His promise is that He will employ us as vessels of honor (2 Timothy 2:20) if we obey.

Can you imagine that—hundreds, thousands of Christians obeying every verse of God's word even when it hurts or looks preposterous?

That's the love of God. That's glory. That's where I want to go.

Do you?